T0178690

Crowdsourcing

FOCUS SERIES

Series Editor Jean-Charles Pomerol

Crowdsourcing

One Step Beyond

Jean-Fabrice Lebraty
Katia Lobre-Lebraty

WILEY

First published 2013 in Great Britain and the United States by ISTE Ltd and John Wiley & Sons, Inc.

ISTE Ltd
27-37 St George's Road
London SW19 4EU
UK

www.iste.co.uk

John Wiley & Sons, Inc.
111 River Street
Hoboken, NJ 07030
USA

www.wiley.com

Library of Congress Control Number: 2013942764

British Library Cataloguing-in-Publication Data
A CIP record for this book is available from the British Library
ISSN: 2051-2481 (Print)
ISSN: 2051-249X (Online)
ISBN: 978-1-84821-466-8

Printed and bound in Great Britain by CPI Group (UK) Ltd., Croydon, Surrey CR0 4YY

Contents

Introduction

This book is intentionally grounded in the field of Management Science; that is, the sciences that seek to understand work in order to improve the functioning of organizations. As recently noted by an esteemed colleague, Professor François-Xavier De Vaujany, during a presentation to support an Authorization to Direct Research (Habilitation à Diriger des Recherches)[1], the sciences of management and sociology fundamentally differ in terms of their subject, though they do share some common points. Sociology examines "how to live together" and Management Science looks at "how to act together". We are, then, clearly in the domain of organized action. More precisely still, we study management situations defined by Girin [GIR 90, p. 142] as:

> "A management situation occurs when participants are brought together and must, in a set amount of time, accomplish a collective action leading to a result subject to an external judgment."

A management situation therefore includes individual actions, but these are integrated into the workings of the organization. Moreover, a result is expected and will be assessed by various stakeholders and major participants [FRE 84] in this organization.

Of course, there are different types of management situations, marked notably by the changes of the economic world within which organizations evolve, in particular the "crisis–opportunity–crisis" loops that have shaped the economic world for 40 years now. In fact,

---

1 January 13, 2013 on the campus of the University of Lyon III.

the first oil shock in 1973 put a definitive end to the glorious 30 years of French economic prosperity, and since then cycles alternating between economic hope and despair have continued to recur. The financial crisis of 2008 is currently being succeeded by a resurgence of optimism, the most visible sign of which is the recent record Dow Jones index: 15,056 on May 7, 2013.

I.1. A typology of management situations

A typology distinguishing four management situations according to two dimensions allows for a better understanding of this concept that is so central for managers, particularly in terms of deployable tools and methods. The first dimension concerns the nature of the environment in the organization within which the management situation occurs. This environment may be considered normal or extreme depending on whether or not it is permanently marked by changeability, uncertainty, and risk for the participants. The second dimension concerns the state of the environment at a given moment. This can be its normal state or a state of crisis according to whether it is undergoing an unusual event. The intersection of these two dimensions therefore allows us to identify four management situations, two aspects of which should be noted: the permeability of the boundaries, which allows passage from one management situation to another; and the increased frequency of passages from one management situation to another, a frequency related particularly to the acceleration of the economic cycles mentioned above.

The four typical management situations can be described as follows:

– The first situation is the so-called normal situation, in which it is possible to apply classic management methods from the 1970s and 1980s (optimization, planning, certification, etc.). In this type of situation, illustrated by the case of a chain restaurant franchise located in a place with high tourist traffic which is not experiencing any specific problems, the occurrence of a minor incident (a client unhappy with his meal, for example) will have little effect on the overall functioning of the restaurant chain.

– The second situation is the so-called crisis situation. It arises when an unusual and impactive event occurs within an organization that generally deals with normal management situations (as described in the preceding paragraph). For example: high pollution leads tourists to abandon the area where the restaurant is located; or: the press reveals a food scandal that directly involves the restaurant chain (these two levels of crisis are obviously different, but they are both crises for the restaurant owner). This crisis situation can be managed using classic crisis management approaches such as those proposed by Lagadec [LAG 91] or Wybo [WYB 04].

– The third situation may be called an "extreme management situation". We consider a management situation to have become extreme when it occurs in an environment permanently marked by high changeability, uncertainty, and significant risks for the participants, whether direct (involving their physical safety) or indirect (if their organization weakens, they are in danger of losing their jobs) [BOU 12; WEI 07]. A trading room in an investment bank, or an aerospace company that conducts in-flight tests of prototype planes, works permanently in extreme situations. This type of organization employs experts who are generally highly resilient. Here, even a tiny grain of sand can rapidly turn a "routine" situation[2] into a crisis situation. The major difference between a crisis occurring in a "normal" environment and one occurring in an "extreme" situation lies in the fact that the participants who are directly involved do not have the same skill levels.

– Finally, the fourth situation is the crisis situation that arises in an extreme environment. "Houston, we have a problem"[3] sums up this situation perfectly. Here, nothing counts but the quality of the people involved; particularly their degree of expertise and level of resilience; and the quality of the organization within which they are working. In the example of Apollo XIII, the ability of the crew to maintain an understanding of the situation and to avoid being carried away by their own emotions was exemplary. On the ground, the ability to think of new strategies and to test them rapidly was also remarkable. The trust

2 For a test pilot, conducting a flight is routine. The term "routine" is in no way used in a pejorative sense.
3 Apollo XIII, April 13, 1970 at 3:07:52 a.m., when an oxygen tank exploded 321,860 km above Earth.

between the flight crew and the ground-control personnel was also a decisive factor. On the other hand, in this context it is not possible to have pre-planned methods or strategies to follow. Those participating in these situations must simply confront them. This involves employing coping strategies as shown by Lazarus [LAZ 00], and only the intrinsic qualities and skills of those involved can increase their chances of survival, though they can in no way guarantee it.

The figure below summarizes these four situations:

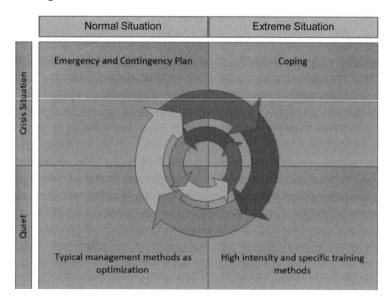

Figure I.1. *Management situations*

I.2. Crowdsourcing: a multifaceted concept

As we will see, crowdsourcing, the subject of analysis in this book, can contribute to the proper functioning of an organization in each of the management situations described above. It can sometimes even constitute *the* innovative solution. A first example of this perspective is that of the recent elections in Kenya. A presidential election was held on March 4, 2013 in this country, which was hardly known for its stability, but which had undergone an unprecedented crisis at the time of its previous election in 2007. During the free election, a fundamental task was to control the regularity of checking the balloting process, particularly through reporting information coming from the thousands of polling stations. During this process, in reaction to the riots provoked by irregularities observed in the Kenyan polling stations in 2007, a platform called Ushahidi was created and provided a partial solution to the problem. In fact, the platform, developed by a young Kenyan named Juliana Rotich, allowed anyone to report an irregularity, either by sending a text message to the number 3002 or by posting a message directly on the platform's website. It was then a matter of correlating the information thus reported with the direct observations of the members of the international observation mission. It is still too early for a complete assessment of this experiment, but the initial results indicate that there does not seem to have been massive fraud.

What can we conclude for now? This is an extreme management situation (marked by changeability, uncertainty, and risk) that involves an extended area (a country the size of France). The task for the organization in charge of monitoring elections and for security officers consists of monitoring the proper functioning of the voting process; this is crucial, as poor functioning can lead to a crisis tipping point. Traditionally, this task is undertaken by investigation teams that are identified, selected, and trained before the election. In this case, these teams were strengthened by a large number of anonymous individuals simply connected to a network. The "anonymous" participation of these masses of people was passionate in nature and deserves emphasis. Paradoxically, trust was placed in the anonymous masses during an electoral process intended to very precisely define the roles of each of them. Moreover, the anonymity of the crowd possessing mobile telephones and microcomputers exercised strong and ubiquitous pressure on the people who would have been tempted to create incidents. Thus, by the very fact of its existence, this experiment can contribute to smooth election processes.

As this example attests, crowdsourcing concerns not only the world of business; its range of applications is much wider. One of this book's objectives is to show the diversity of crowdsourcing by attempting an exhaustive recapitulation of all its forms[4] and defining its specific attributes. The case of Innocentive alone shows some of the confusion present around crowdsourcing and some of the forms it may take in matters of Research and Development (R&D). It has often been said that the Innocentive platform can provide a company with the means to externalize its R&D department. This is not entirely true; though Innocentive does allow the externalization of a small percentage of an organization's R&D activities, particularly those that can be formalized with precision, in fact, only problems that are clearly identified and formalized can be submitted to the masses via Innocentive. The work done by Innocentive stems from a specific form of crowdsourcing, "crowdsourcing and innovation", which allows an organization to benefit from the specialized expertise of individuals spread out all over the globe in order to solve identified and timely problems. The mission of an R&D department is not limited to this single type of problem; it also consists, for example, of identifying these same problems, and of creating and conceiving new goods and services in accordance with the business's environment. There are consequently other forms of crowdsourcing that can be mobilized, including "crowdauditing", "crowd and forecasting", and "crowdsourcing and authenticity". It appears that only the combined use of various forms of crowdsourcing would allow an organization to externalize a large portion of its R&D department.

Now, though, let us look back at a page from the history of the world of organizations, by outlining the context and, in particular, two major trends within which crowdsourcing emerged. Since 1995, the year of Netscape's IPO[5] and the mass diffusion of the Internet, two major paradoxes characterizing the organizational environment have been at work: the coexistence of rarity and abundance, and the simultaneity of crisis and opposition to change.

---

4 However, the daring nature of the objective should be emphasized, insofar as crowdsourcing is a phenomenon in full expansion and its limits, in conjunction with the combined power of the Web and the masses, are difficult to define in principle. There is every reason to believe that new forms of crowdsourcing will appear between the submission of this book to our publisher and its appearance in bookstores.
5 Initial Public Offer: date on which Netscape went public on the stock market.

Acknowledgments

We would like to thank all those brilliant people with brilliant ideas who have inspired us to write this book. We think of academics and entrepreneurs as students navigating the sea of crowdsourcing. Special thanks to those at the universities of Lyon and in Lausanne, Paris, and Nice, as well as overseas (China and the Middle East).

It is true that the crowdsourcing movement is an ongoing process propelling us toward a new world of business opportunities but – and this is key – there is an element of fun that goes along with it. It is this joyful aspect that puts us in mind of Camden Town market in London, and the lyrics we used to sing along with there: "One step beyond..."

A Turbulent and Paradoxical Environment

The 1990s were the start of a new era, marked by two major revolutions: the advent of economic financialization, and the mass diffusion of the Internet.

1.1. Economic financialization and its challenges

In his latest book, Gomez [GOM 13] offers an original analysis of economic financialization and the manner in which it is manifested in the behavior of businesses. We have based this writing on his analysis. The roots of economic financialization lie in the investment of savings by households which, desirous of preserving these savings, aspire to the security and liquidity of their investments. This is what is offered to them by the finance industry, which transmutes household savings into financial products such as SICAVs (*Société d'Investissement à Captial Variable,* "investment company with variable capital"), common investment funds, and life insurance products. The finance industry's task is to place the resources collected in safe and profitable investments: safe, so that the savings are not lost in risky business ventures; and profitable, so that the profits earned, rather than the businesses' capital, procure a profit for the savers in the form of dividends. From this perspective, household savings are directed mainly toward large companies that are listed on the stock market.

The stock market, as a second-hand sharemarket, ensures the liquidity of investments; the preference given to large companies is justified by their perceived economic stability: they are considered "too big to fail". What occurs next is a phenomenon of attraction: the more capital businesses obtain, the more they become interesting investment targets for funds. Because they are powerful and their capital is liquid, they attract new investments. Money attracts money.

There has also been unprecedented competition between these large listed companies, which secure and seek to secure household savings. They must in fact attract the large-scale attention of backers by producing the expected profit and by clearing at least as large a profit as their competitors do. Therefore, companies outdo each other to prove the merits of their use of the capital they seek to obtain. In other words, they mimic each other in order to fulfill what they see as the market's expectations of them. These common projected expectations include the imagined market requirement of 15% profit on the capital invested; the speed with which the critical profit margin must be reached; and the necessity of becoming global, or of maintaining flexibility. The means chosen to achieve these objectives are as similar as the objectives themselves. They include innovation, business mergers, strategic international growth, and development of sophisticated managerial monitoring and reporting tools. These tools are intended to note, via the power of computer information systems, how each activity contributes (or does not contribute) to the final result, thus   rationalizing the activities of these organizations. The result is that the organizations have been put under increasing pressure: large listed companies most of all, but also other companies, partners, clients, suppliers, and subcontractors, on whom the large companies put a great deal of pressure to achieve their own objectives.

Finally, and in an exaggerated manner, a direct link can be established between the savings of millions of small and anonymous households, and the mimetic behavior of thousands of large and small businesses under intense pressure in an ever-more competitive environment.

1.2. The mass diffusion of the Internet and its consequences

Though they are often cited, we believe that the massive transformations engendered by information technology remain under-evaluated. However, in his book, Friedman [FRI 05] emphasized the driving role of the Internet in global evolution. Remember that, above all, what we call the Internet is really a consolidation of various information technologies, some of which do not yet use the Internet protocol (text messages and Blackberry messages, for example). A piece of technology consists of a technique and a useful logic (techno + logic); there are many techniques or applications (the Web, Skype, Twitter, Peer to Peer, videos, newsgroups etc.) and various ways of using them. Understanding the distinction between technique and logic is very important. A mobile telephone[1], for example, is not necessarily a tool used to exchange voice communications over a long distance[2]; it can often be a short-range coordination tool[3], as in "I'll be there in 2 minutes. I'm here, can you see me?". It is also important not to confuse these terms: the Internet is a protocol and the Web, for example, is an application that uses this protocol. The headline of the August 2010 issue of *Wired* magazine clearly showed this nuance: "The Web is Dead. Long Live the Internet". This showed that the Web was no longer the dominant application for the enduringly dynamic protocol that is the Internet.

Let us look at two examples.

On September 15, 2008, the Lehman Brothers investment bank went bankrupt after 150 years in existence. This failure was rooted in a panic that drove investors to withdraw their money at the same time. Banks cannot survive this type of situation since they do not possess enough ready cash. Certainly, to ensure their clients' trust, they invest money in securities that are liquid enough – that is, easy to resell in the case of mass client withdrawals. However, this liquidity has limits, the exceeding of which is statistically controlled in a confidence-based situation. They also invest the savings entrusted to them in diverse securities in order to ensure the safety of the investments. How then to

---

1 Technical component.
2 Logic component.
3 Another logic component.

explain the crisis of confidence around Lehman Brothers? Where did the panic come from, and why had no one foreseen it? Information technology played a role in this bankruptcy; should it also play a role in avoiding such a situation?

Another example can be found in the numerous movements that have rattled the Arab world for the last four years. These have demonstrated a massive use of communication tools; whether in private communications within groups, local coordination or the diffusion of images or propaganda, all of the participants have used these technologies. These technologies are not the source of the movements, but the role of lever played by them is undeniable. The way in which social movements both act and react on the Internet thus requires the development of new models of analysis.

The lesson we can draw from these two examples is that it is becoming nearly impossible to have a precise image of a situation. The dynamic of technology blurs this image by causing it to evolve continually. Without clear visibility, it becomes impossible to predict the future, even in the short term. Yet classic methods of data analysis and prediction continue to dominate managerial thinking.

Technology has come to play more than a paradoxical role. On the one hand, as we have noted, it makes situations more unpredictable. In fact, the participation of individuals in network activities has passed a threshold [GLA 00] and this human–technology blend of information destabilizes existing models. On the other hand, their ever-increasing capabilities are leading to the development of extremely powerful systems of analysis. The concepts, which we will discuss, of Big Data and Open Data, for example, have recently borne witness to the development of these capabilities, and three subsequent articles in the *Harvard Business Review* perfectly illustrate this resurgence of analysis [BAR 12; MAR 13; WIL 12].

1.3. The paradoxical coexistence of scarcity and abundance around data

Very large volumes of data are being produced today by both individuals and organizations. This production is the result of an ever-increasing use of communication resources in permanent interaction with the information systems of multiple organizations. The growing use of the Internet comes to mind, as does the ubiquity of mobile telephones, which today allow the whole world to be connected via telephone media, but also via mobile Internet accessible by Smartphones. Even without dwelling on the booming industry of all sorts of sensors for capturing data of every type[4], which frequently interact with, and provide useful information to, organizations, the list of the principal "producers/generators" of data remains largely incomplete.

These large volumes of data pose multiple questions to the organizations that collect and/or generate them, due in particular to their size, diversity, and the resources that must be implemented in order to exploit them; this is what we call Big Data (BD). There is consensus on one point concerning this data, and that is the vast potential it possesses with regard to the analysis of political opinions[5] or industrial trends[6], epidemiology, or the fight against criminality[7], to cite just a few examples. With skill and the appropriately adapted computer resources used in its capture, storage, processing, and analysis, this data can give us direct access to the reality of physical or social phenomena that have been out of reach until now. That is why Big Data is regarded today by some as the new scientific revolution [MCA 12].

Open Data (OD) is a phenomenon connected to Big Data. Here, an organization makes some of its data freely available via the Web so that it can be reused by private individuals and/or businesses.

The OD phenomenon is the result of a double (r)evolution:

– Technical, with the exponential growth in volume of digitized data (Big Data) and the collaborative nature of the Web 2.0.

---

4 Data on weather, pollution levels, the frequentation of a communication channel, etc.
5 http://123opendata.com/blog/big-data-campagne-presidentielle-us/.
6 http://lecercle.lesechos.fr/entreprises-marches/high-techmedias/internet/221144150/big-data-adn-utilisateur-sequencable-moins-1.
7 http://www.lemagit.fr/technologie/securite-technologie/2012/03/12/la-eacute-curit-eacute-met-eacute-solument-laquo-big-data-raquo/.

– Political, since the OD movement is supported by most Western governments, led by those of the United Kingdom and the United States.[8]

More precisely, OD was born in the United Kingdom in 2009, the brainchild of Tim Berners Lee, the principal inventor of the Web, who envisioned switching from Web 2.0 to government 2.0. It can be defined as the use of Web 2.0 collaborative tools to make a government, via its administrations, more open, transparent, collaborative, responsive, and efficient. It is simultaneously motivated by a new democratic momentum based on the restoration of public data to the citizens who actually own it, and by the development of a new culture based on efficiency thanks to the exploitation of resources (open public data) that were previously used mostly or entirely internally.

We can see today a generalization of the release of public data on a geographical level[9]. These public projects share the same objectives of democratic transparency, participation, citizen involvement, and economic development. For example, on April 11, 2012, the ANACT network (*Agence Nationale pour l'Amélioration des Conditions de Travail*, "French national agency for the improvement of working conditions"), which is aimed at improving work conditions, made a group of interactive maps available to Internet readers. The objective of this data is to better understand various work contexts, so that potential users can suggest solutions adapted to these contexts.

The OD movement is spreading geographically, but it is also gaining ground in the private sector:

– via companies acting by order of public service, who are therefore affected by the legal obligation to data openness, such as the Suez environmental group or the RATP[10], for example;

---

8 Note that after some hesitation, France opened its sole interministerial public data portal, data.gouv.fr, on December 5, 2011.

9 It has even been made obligatory in France via European directives and national legislation, as an opposable law.

10 French public transport operator, *Régie Autonome des Transports Parisiens* (Autonomous Operator of Parisian Transport).

– but also, and especially, as part of a voluntaristic strategy on the part of private companies, a strategy related to the analysis of opportunities in terms of business, image or innovation (we may cite, for example, the SNCF [11] in France, or the Poult group, which specializes in manufacturing cookies, as a distributor brand) [BLU 11].

The data released by organizations is intended to be used by individuals or other organizations. To this end, OD compiles large volumes of available data whose potential lies, particularly via Big Data, in the development of new businesses founded on the basis of this data. However, in addition to the issues specific to Big Data (capture, storage, processing, and analysis of very large volumes of data, etc.), there are issues specific to OD. These are organizational in nature, presuppose that organizations determine their objectives in matters of OD, and assess the risks associated with it. It is only in this way that they can choose the data they will release (with or without rights) and that they will know how to define the procedures relative to the opening of this data. They must also learn to manage the collaboration with communities of users in order to attract private citizens, interested individuals, associations, journalists and researchers, and incite them to manipulate this data in order to draw from it new applications and new services and to create value [LEB 10]. It is a matter, then, of these organizations developing new skills. OD also raises technical questions, since the data must be cleaned up and redesignated before it is released. It raises legal questions as well, with the current coexistence of various types of data-protection license regulating the use, particularly the commercial use, of public data. Finally, it raises societal questions around the democratic functioning of governments and the risks of drifting related to a "safe" use of this Big Data, or a "populist" use in the analysis of data by unscrupulous individuals [LOB 12].

In order to keep their promises, such as the improvement of client satisfaction, for example, the development of an ecosystem of partners and the sped-up market release of new offers in accordance with consumer expectations, BD and OD assume heavy investments. The

---

11 French public railway company, *Société Nationale des Chemins de fer Français* (National society of French railways).

resource constituted by this abundance of data will remain only potential, unless it is accompanied by human skill and the hardware and software necessary to manage it. The human skill aspect is particularly important, since in order to process this data, the experts must have highly specialized skills combining information technology, statistics, and big business, which are rare indeed. On the hardware/software side, the Big Data market is in the process ofstructuralization, currently bringing together important players such as Oracle, IBM, EMC, Informatica, and Microsoft, which offer solutions based on the Hadoop open source model[12], as well as start-ups, since with the computing cloud, which allows for powerful access to storage and processing on demand, companies no longer have to be large in order to work on large masses of data.

Here, we see the paradox of scarcity and abundance that exists around this data. Information systems have not been spared the budgetary reductions stemming from the increasing pressure placed on organizations, yet the ever-tighter competitive environment requires ongoing improvements in competitiveness and efficiency. The result of this is a reduction in the margins of organizational maneuvering. These margins, also called *organizational slack* [RIC 10], play a fundamental role when organizations undertake new endeavors such as BD and OD. In fact, these solutions may appear to be flourishing, but their emerging nature requires room to maneuver for the inevitable and necessary trial and error.

1.4. Unique simultaneity of crisis and immobilism

The crisis that began in 2008 and is still affecting the entire global economy no longer requires proof. Its consequences in Europe and particularly in France remain weighty. In addition, the observation of a certain kind of immobilism of companies in the face of this crisis situation seems particularly surprising. To illustrate this immobilism, we will look at four sectors that appear to be experiencing difficulties

---

12 Apache Hadoop is an open-source software framework that supports data-intensive distributed applications, licensed under the Apache v2 license. It supports the running of applications on large clusters of commodity hardware. Hadoop was derived from Google MapReduce and Google File System (GFS) papers.

in generating business relationships with their crowds: the banking, postal, and television sectors, and finally the training sector in the case of universities.

1.4.1. *The online banking sector*

To date in France there has been no independent retail bank existing solely online. In view of this, we will try to understand more clearly why such an activity (retail banking) has not been the subject of major innovations over the past decade. It is indeed surprising to read, in a 1997 issue of the newapaper *Les Echos*, the following sentence calling the development of the Internet:

> "An evolution that has not escaped the French establishments, which are beginning to explore the Internet, following the example of Banque Direct (www.banquedirecte.fr)." [DEJ 97]

In 2013 the exploration continues, but it seems that this is a sector particularly favorable to virtual relationships.

First of all, it should be noted that the activities of a retail bank are perfectly suited to online processing, particularly for the reasons below:

– Currency in itself is a more and more dematerialized and universal concept, as a transfer of €1,000 between France and Finland bears witness.

– Products and services are themselves intangible (a credit or an investment in a savings product is a virtual activity).

– The advising aspect does not seem to require a wealth of information, since it involves only face-to-face relationships.

– The opening hours of banks are the same as those of a standard work day; it is not a given for a client to go and see his/her banking advisor.

Next, banks aim at reaching a large number of people of all ages. Young people are targeted as future clients as well. Thus, initiatives to ensure their loyalty are multiplying (sponsorship, free credit cards, etc.). Older individuals are also being offered adapted services, such as retirement services. Professionals are courted as well, particularly via customized credit. Moreover, in early April 2013 the Crédit Mutuel site offered three login points: young people, private individuals, and professionals.

Finally, banks rely on a solid computer architecture which, even though it is often externalized, remains sturdy. Banks also have a certain capital of trust in terms of their ability not to make mistakes or commit criminal acts (compared to relationships with private individuals).

Yet, in mid-2013, innovations of separation in the banking domain are hardly perceptible, and the following questions remain without a concrete response:

– How can increased client volume be used to generate business activity other than the traditional banking activity?

– How can traditional banking/insurance activity be developed using the resource of the diversity of client skills?

– Who will be able to compete with a major social networking entity (such as Facebook) when Facebook begins offering ways to make virtual payments?

– What are the responses to a service like Paypal?

– Why have physical offices?

In the face of these questions, which are general in nature but of capital importance for banks, the only responses given have been classic externalizations, particularly those of computer services. None of the responses involve turning to the client crowd, or a true virtualization of the relationship.

1.4.2. *The postal sector*

The blossoming of e-commerce has been relatively slow in France, but it has accelerated considerably since 2007. Let us look at the case of a company specializing in the private sale of "remaindered" goods.[13] This company has exceeded €2 billion profit for more than two years, and for some brands there are more than 1 million people registered, and 470,000 products have been sold in a single stroke. Obviously, these products need to be dispatched. The internal, logistical aspect of private sale seems extremely costly, since a service provider must deliver the products to their buyers. This single example illustrates the immense opportunity for the postal sector that is constituted by this online commerce. Yet, at least in France, separation innovations in the area of parcel delivery are difficult to find. However, more than 15 years ago, Nicholas Negroponte was already suggesting the installation of refrigerators at building entrances to facilitate the night-time delivery of fresh products. This excellent idea has yet to be implemented. There has been no taking into account the possibilities of crowd participation and implementation. This is unfortunate, as all the ingredients are present:

– Most parcels do not require any particular skill in their handling.

– Tracking and traceability technologies (mainly radio frequency identification (RFID) and barcodes).

– Enormous need: there are huge numbers of parcels to transport as effectively as possible.

This second example clearly shows the existence of opportunities that have not yet been seized.

1.4.3. *The television sector*

This 1-to-N mass diffusion media is universally deployed. It is a sector which, particularly in France, was constructed in a traditional manner with organizations externalizing few tasks. The development of the Internet then led this sector to evolve, and budgetary constraints in particular motivated the development of partnerships with well-identified service providers (production companies, photo agencies, etc.). The simultaneous development of globalization also had an immense impact; indeed, it has become impossible for a channel to retain a dense network of reporters ready to supply information about

---

13 https://secure.fr.vente-privee.com/.

events liable to occur all over the globe. The competition posed by sites like YouTube is also very strong. Reporting of high technical quality has been replaced by jerky images filmed with mobile telephones. Unlike the two previous examples, television channels including France 24 very quickly came to rely on more or less well-identified individuals for the provision of content. France 24's network of observers now numbers several thousand people who send reports each day which the channel's editorial service then verifies and decides whether or not to broadcast.This initiative shows that it is possible, and even highly pertinent, to use the crowd in pursuing its principal activity. However, this example also emphasizes a certain restraint in the use of the crowd. In reality, it accounts for only a slight percentage of the reports broadcast, and the decision to broadcast is made solely by the television channel's directorate.

1.4.4. *The training sector: French universities*

The eight-century-old French university system has developed in fits and starts; often a worldwide leader, it also occasionally lags behind. Once again, the development of technologies both has constitued and does constitute a source of profound evolution. New competitors are arriving while old ones disappear, and above all, new ways of teaching are emerging. Long-distance learning, also called e-learning, is a theme that became fashionable between 1995 and 2000. It should be noted that the confidential nature of this type of learning was retained in France. However, today, all of the elements are in place for the development of a commercial training offer based on this remote approach. Indeed, the example of the course on Artificial Intelligence given by Professor Thrun of the University of Standford, which attracted nearly 160,000 students, is a highly alarming sign.[14] A viable business model should not be too hard to find. Would a French student not be ready to pay €500 to have an online degree from MIT? And (160,000 x 500) = 80,000,000 – quite a tidy overall profit.

---

14 These are called MOOCs (Massive Open Online Courses). The EDx initiative launched by Harvard and MIT is also beginning to bring out new ideas for the future of long-distance learning.

1.4.5. *The conclusion to be drawn from these cases: the crowd remains an underexploited resource*

This point, based on four examples (banking, the postal sector, television and universities) shows that in the current context, an organization faces major challenges. To date, the principal solutions envisioned have been classic externalization and outsourcing; but these classic management methods have reached their limits. Organizations are evolving in extreme situations; that is, situations that can rapidly turn into crisis situations. These organizations cannot keep eternally improving their efficiency using classic methods; they need to find new ideas and new resources. It seems necessary to find new opportunities for potential customer bases as well. Like other researchers [BOU 13], we believe the crowd is one of these. It may prove to be a major resource, particularly for organizations that have access to a widely-connected crowd that often wishes only to participate. In the four illustrations we have shown (crowd x technology) = creation of opportunities. However, the implementation of methods to benefit from these opportunities is no simple matter. In this, a deep understanding of the concept of crowdsourcing and the attentive observation of new companies using this opportunity may constitute a source of inspiration leading to the overcoming of the crisis-immobilism paradox.

2

Crowdsourcing: A New Form of Externalization

The goal of this chapter is to explain exactly what is meant by the term "crowdsourcing". We will discuss various definitions of crowdsourcing and review related concepts such as outsourcing, relationships, and the crowd.

Open source, open innovation, open externalization, or crowdsourcing: where will this trend of organizational opening end? Four factors are at work in this phenomenon: calculation power (computers, smartphone tablets, many other devices); digitized data and information; a universal network protocol (Internet); and, above all, individuals connected to each other. Anderson [AND 12] specifies that in these conditions, elements will circulate and be copied and recopied, as well as sometimes changed. These modifications, made possible by the characteristics of the technology, will enrich the initial element with diverse perspectives and experiences, thus turning it into a new and unique element. Sometimes, however, a modification is no longer just incremental; it becomes a disruptive innovation [DOW 13]. Recall that we define a disruptive or radical innovation[1] as the act of offering a product, service or process that is radically new for a given sector. There are many cases of radical innovations, such

---

[1] Though some differentiate between disruptive and radical, here we simply place incremental and radical or disruptive on opposing sides.

as the startup Zynga, which is an online games platform that has developed a virtual currency [PET 12]. In our opinion, crowdsourcing as a global phenomenon also constitutes a disruptive innovation.

Wired magazine is well-known to the worldwide information technology community. Founded 20 years ago, numerous ideas have been introduced in this magazine, including the potentialities of open source in November 2003. New concepts have also appeared there first, such as "long tail" [AND 06]. It was in this magazine as well, in June 2006, that Howe [HOW 06] proposed the term "crowdsourcing" in reference to a new method of externalization.

Several definitions of the concept of crowdsourcing have been suggested and are listed in the table below.

Definition	Author
Crowdsourcing is the act of outsourcing tasks to an undefined, large group of people, through an open call.	[HOW 08] http://www.youtube.com/watch?v=F0-UtNg3ots
Crowdsourcing is channeling the experts' desire to solve a problem and then freely sharing the answer with everyone.	[VAN 10] http://fr.slideshare.net/searchbistro/harvesting-knowledge-how-to-crowdsource-in-2010
We say that a system is a crowdsourcing system if it enlists a crowd of humans to help solve a problem defined by the system owners, and if in doing so, it addresses the following four fundamental challenges: How to recruit and retain users? What contributions can users make? How to combine user contributions to solve the target problem? How to evaluate users and their contributions?	[DOA 11] http://cacm.acm.org/magazines/2011/4/106563-crowdsourcing-systems-on-the-world-wide-web/fulltext
Crowdsourcing is a neologism for the act of taking tasks traditionally performed by an employee or contractor, and outsourcing it to an undefined, generally large group of people or a community in the form of an open call.	[BEL 09]

Howe's definition seems to us to be the most illustrative; we would alter it slightly to read:

> "Crowdsourcing is the externalization by an organization, via an application using the Internet protocol, of an activity to a large number of individuals whose identities are most often anonymous."

We will now define the terms used in this definition.

2.1. The concept of externalization

Externalization has become a major method of governing the activities of an organization. It is an agreement that stipulates that an organization will have part of the activities for which it is responsible carried out by another organization. A contract formalizes the details of transfer of the activity. Arnold [ARN 00] proposes a model based on four components characterizing an externalization:

– The organization making the strategic decision to externalize.

– The activities to be externalized. Four types of activities can be distinguished (activities constituting the core of the job; activities directly linked to the core activities of the job; support activities; and secondary activities).

– The organizations assuming responsibility for these externalized activities, commonly called suppliers.

– The form taken by the externalization; more particularly its intensity, also called the degree of externalization, which harkens back to the concept of hybrid organization. We also refer to "hybrid governance structure" in the transaction cost theory [COA 37; WIL 85]. This concept of hybridity raises the question of organizational boundaries.

From our point of view, these four components can also be used to characterize a crowdsourcing operation, with the slight difference that the suppliers are not organizations, but individuals emerging from the crowd of Internet users.

It is the call on an anonymous crowd rather than on a pre-selected supplier which, in the definition we are using, differentiates crowdsourcing most fundamentally from outsourcing. Moreover, [LEB 09] suggests the term "open externalization" for the new concept, with the double intention of:

– Differentiating crowdsourcing from "classic" externalization to a previously identified and selected organization corresponding to a "closed externalization".

– Expressing the spirit behind this concept, which is similar to the spirit prevalent in the world of "open-source" software [GOS 03].

2.2. The idea of relationships

Crowdsourcing necessarily involves a relationship between the externalizing organization and the individual who accepts the externalized task via the Web.

The following criteria can be used to define a relationship:

– The number of actors. Relationships can take the classic forms: 1-1, 1-n, n-1 and n-n. In the context of crowdsourcing, the initial relationship has the form 1-n. Then, once the individual has been selected from the crowd, the relationship changes to 1-1, which will be multiplied according to the needs of the crowdsourcing operation. In other words, the organization will be in a relationship x times with an individual.

– Intensity of the relationship – strong bonds and weak bonds.

– Duration of the relationship.

– Anonymity of the relationship.

An important point in these relationships is the idea of trust.

The concept of trust is the subject of many studies in Management Science. Multiple visions of trust exist, but they all begin with the postulate that trust emerges from uncertain and risky situations. For example, in 1958 M. Deutsch presented trust as:

"[T]he act of relying on the characteristics of an object, the probability of an event, or the behavior of a person, with the goal of attaining a desired but uncertain objective, in the context of a risky situation." [DEU 58]

Trust can be described according to two epistemological postures [SMY 10]. First, a positivist approach stipulating that trust is an important component of any relationship. In this case, trust constitutes a factor that is important but only one of many to be taken into account, and which can be measured. Second, from a more interpretive perspective, trust constitutes the very foundation of the relationship and will therefore grow and evolve in the manner of the relationship itself. In agreement with Rousseau *et al.* [ROU 98], Edkinks and Smyth suggest the following definition:

"Trust is a disposition and attitude concerning the willingness to rely upon the actions of or be vulnerable towards another party, under circumstances of contractual and social obligations, with the potential for collaboration." [EDK 06]

We would add that there is a strong link between confidence and the truthfulness of the message [ROD 10].

2.3. The concept of a crowd

In his book, which has gone through many editions, G. Le Bon [LEB 03] states:

"[T]he word "crowd" represents a coming-together of any individuals, no matter what the chances are that cause them to gather." (p. 2)

This definition seems broad; however, Le Bon immediately adds that:

"[F]rom a psychological point of view, the term "crowd" takes on another meaning entirely. In certain circumstances, and only in these circumstances, an agglomeration of people possesses new and very different characteristics than those of each individual that makes it up."

He then invokes the idea of the "organized crowd".

We are then faced with a variable sum game. Sometimes the sum can be negative, in the event that the crowd's behavior leans toward values that are considered negative, such as baseness or violence. Sometimes the sum is positive, and that is the case in which we are interested here. In his book, J. Surowiecki [SUR 05] stipulates that two elements are required for the constitution of a sensible crowd. The first element is diversity of interpretation. With varied individual and/or group skills, individuals will give varying meanings to a single fact or question. This is an important point, as it leads to differentiating a crowd that may refer to itself as a community from the concept of a community of practices [LEF 04]. A community of practices implies a certain homogeneity of ways of doing things and of attitudes and ways of thinking, which tends to reduce diversity. The preponderant role assigned to diversity also raises an important question: what is the minimum number of people required for a group to be considered a crowd? J. Howe suggests the figure 5,000 [HOW 09, p. 282], but no scientific basis has been demonstrated. What has been shown is that within a crowd there are "quality circles" that lead to 90% of the crowd suggesting useless ideas, 9% interesting ideas, and 1% very interesting ideas, and that it is expected that one ε will strike on a brilliant idea.

Beyond the differences between members of a crowd, a crowdsourcing operation may produce a feeling of ubiquity, since the crowd is everywhere. Thus, and we have observed this during our many discussions with actors in this world, the entrepreneur who turns to crowdsourcing often feels as if he/she belongs to a global group; as if he is in several places at the same time. The following types of reaction confirm this sense:

> "There's even one guy who's in Armenia...and another one in Argentina...oh yes, and there was a Filipino who came up with a really great idea..."

To better understand the idea of a crowd, we must ask ourselves about its behavior. It is also important to remember that calling on a crowd does not preclude the use of a group of well-identified experts. As we will see, there can be a complementary dynamic between a crowd and a group of experts around a single activity.

2.3.1. *The connected crowd*

It is impossible to think of a "connected crowd" in 2013 without doing so in the context of social networks. Since 2005, social network systems (SNS) have spread all over the globe and been adopted by Internet users with a speed unparalleled in information technology. In less than 8 years, 12% of the world's population has created an account on the social networking site Facebook, and as of April 2010 almost 100% of American students had a Facebook account. This technology has also gone hand-in-hand with certain social and political changes in emerging countries, and its role was widely emphasized in the Arab revolution of 2011, for example. Since social networking sites now act as containers constantly incorporating more connection-related services, it has become impossible to avoid them, as Marc Zuckerberg recently stated[2], and it is this idea that we pass on to our students: "Being on a social network has its dangers, but not being on one is suicidal."

With regard to organizations, the use of these social networks is not neutral. Because social network technology makes information visible that was previously hidden within the organization, this technology can lead to the destabilization of an organization [STA 99]. Most organizations are structured hierarchically with formal procedures. By bringing to light the informal relationships within the organization, social network technology changes the representation of the organizational structure by emphasizing collaborative practices and interdepartmental exchanges. This new representation can lead to changes in work practices. For example, it may incite actors to free themselves from hierarchical sequences and to prioritize direct contact between actors. Here, there is an

---

2 http://www.theverge.com/2013/3/7/4075822/facebook-wants-to-be-the-social-network-of-record.

opportunity for actors to redefine their areas of uncertainty and to start the social game of the organization over from scratch [CRO 77]. Beyond this, the sharing of new information about the organization of work can lead to the consideration of new elements of distinction and comparison between actors. The whole system may then be judged by its actors as inequitable. For example, actors who are led in the execution of their tasks to work in collaboration with other services may become part of an extended social network within the organization, while others whose tasks are confined to one department will not necessarily be able to do this. Therefore, the visibility of the social network for each person will not benefit all of the actors in an organization equally. Some of these actors will then be hesitant to use the system to protect their own interests and social position within the company, while others, on the contrary, will promote the system, since it gives them the opportunity to define a new social position for themselves. Finally, since these technologies are simple to use and their functioning is based on the individual personal data that actors agree to declare, individuals are free to share what they wish via social networking technology. As with the social networks present on the Web [CAR 08], actors can develop strategies within their organization to manage and make their social capital visible. They can choose not to show their entire social network in the system, or they may decide to self-promote and to share all of the types of links they have established. The use of social networks as part of crowdsourcing operations constitutes a true opportunity for connection. However, as we have just noted, this technology is not neutral, either in terms of internal actor strategies or in terms of the outside relationships to which it contributes – that is, the relationship with the crowd. Among the questions raised by this absence of neutrality is that of the diversity and independence of the members of a crowd when this crowd enters into a relationship with an organization via a social network.

In addition to social network technologies, forming close relationships between various actor constitutes the very essence of the Internet. The job market sector is a perfect illustration of this connection-related research. A site such as Irantalent bears witness to the need of businesses and graduates to connect with each other.

The traditional manner of characterizing a relationship is based on the work of Granovetter [GRA 73]. The ideas of strong bonds and weak bonds were widely applied in research on the world of social networking and the connection of actors via the Internet [CHA 12]. However, the nature of these bonds is based mainly on face-to-face relationships or mediated by basic technologies, principally the telephone. The development of the Internet and of the ability to make exchanges without regard for physical distance or even language barriers has enriched Granovetter's initial approach. More than ever, the strength of weak bonds is making itself felt. In the domain of crowdsourcing, we will see that certain operations are based on the development of strong bonds, while others multiply weak bonds in order to access networks that are far-flung and rich in ideas.

2.3.2. Understanding the crowd

The desire to understand and identify a crowd is often expressed by crowdsourcing actors. Yet it contains a paradox within itself. In fact, it is the diversity and independence of the members of a crowd that leads to the addition of value in a crowdsourcing operation. If one wishes to know the individual members, it is with the intention of selecting them in order to improve the performance of the crowdsourcing operation. This is a deceptively attractive idea to benefit from the richness of the crowd, and it is what we observe when we note that crowdsourcing is on average more successful than controlled methods (consumer panels, representative samples for a survey, or even groups of experts). When a crowd is called upon, honing it down to obtain a sample actually makes it a poorer resource. Should we conclude, then, that organizations should remain passive in the constitution of the crowds for their crowdsourcing operations? Of course not. There are two types of action that can be taken:

– Guaranteeing the independence of the members of the crowd.

– Attempting to predict or determine the overall behavior of the crowd in order to be able to stimulate it.

In order to attempt to understand the mechanisms of a crowd, the approach that seems most interesting to us is derived from epidemiology and from the study of the development of an illness

[KER 11]. Nine characteristics can be identified, whose counterparts in the world of crowdsourcing are shown in the table below.

Epidemiological condition	Perspective of the crowd participating in a crowdsourcing operation
S: susceptible to contamination. For example, a person is susceptible to catching the flu.	An Internet user is susceptible to participation in a crowdsourcing operation.
I: infected. The person has caught the illness.	The Internet user participates in the operation.
R: recovered. The person has recovered. Either he/she has received care, or he/she recovered by him/herself.	The Internet user is no longer participating in the crowdsourcing operation.
E: exposed. The period during which a person is exposed to an illness or the incubation of the illness.	This criterion can be the duration of the media campaign to recruit Internet users or the average time spent by a person near a media outlet diffusing information about the crowdsourcing operation. This can of course be time spent on the Internet, but it can also be time spent watching television if an advertising campaign is launched jointly, or word of mouth, and thus the time a person spends talking to others.
M: immunity. This is the fact that some people possess antibodies that make them immune to the illness.	Certain people may be indifferent to crowdsourcing-type operations or to the type of product proposed by the operation.
Rx: reproduction number. This is the threshold that determines whether or not an epidemic will develop or disappear.	The equivalent of this threshold determines whether the community participating in the crowdsourcing operation will grow or dissipate.
VT: vector transmission. This is the vector of the illness (mosquitoes, contact, etc.)	This is the media used; thus E and VT are very closely linked.

Vaccines: vaccination operations result in an increased number of immunized people.	Certain events can "vaccinate" Internet users against participation in a crowdsourcing operation. For example, if a hoax were introduced on a site such as Innocentive, many internauts sensitive to this type of operation would hesitate to participate again, even on another site.
NHM: non-homogeneous mixing. This means that within a given population, there are distinct subgroups that have different properties in terms of infection.	In the Internet user community, subgroups can also be identified. It may be interesting to profile them in order to better predict which ones will be attracted to a crowdsourcing operation.

Table 2.1. *Epidemiology and crowdsourcing*

At first glance the metaphor seems to hold up, even though it has been applied to the evolution of computer viruses [WAN 13]. However, the objectives being pursued in epidemiology and in crowdsourcing are opposed to one another. In epidemiology, an attempt is made to limit the diffusion of an illness, while in crowdsourcing we try to extend the diffusion of an operation. That being said, the development of an illness and participation in a crowdsourcing operation appear to us to have adequately comparable characteristics (see Table 2.1) to warrant attempting to use them by adapting the epidemiological model to crowdsourcing operations.

There are a large number of possible combinations leading to various epidemiological models; here is one example:

$$S \rightarrow I \rightarrow R$$

(Susceptible to contamination/Infected/Recovered)

Transposed to crowdsourcing, this means that a person is liable to participate in a crowdsourcing operation, then participates in it and finally ends his/her participation.

As discussed on Connor Classen Behan's blog[3], we can represent the curves of individuals S, I and R according to a time scale.

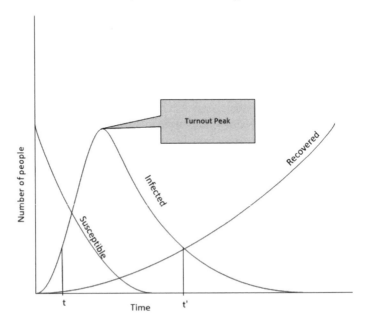

Figure 2.1. *Evolution of a crowd according to an SIR model*

In such a case, we can see clearly that crowdsourcing is only profitable between t and t'. If we measure the audiences and model participation, we can then refer to certain models and in this way predict when the crowdsourcing operation should be stopped.

This is as yet an unexplored area, but one that should be of great interest to managers and researchers.

2.3.3. *Crowds and experts*

It would be wrong to believe that in crowdsourcing there is nothing but the crowd. Alongside the crowd, there are the experts. By "expert", we mean in this case a person or group designated as such

---

3 http://www.smallperturbation.com/.

by the organization, who carries out the crowdsourcing operation. Expertise is a social status granted by an entourage. In our case, the designated expert may be, for example, an independent team responsible for verifying the feasibility of a solution proposed by an individual in the crowd as part of a crowdsourcing operation.

The table below shows the intersection of crowd and expert, with the two principal operations that can be conducted within a crowdsourcing operation: generation and selection of content [4], allowing us to be more precise and to define more clearly the role of each.

	Crowd	*Expert*
Content Generation	1	2
Content Selection	3	4

Table 2.2. *Crowd and expert in a crowdsourcing operation*

These four cases specify "who carries out which operation". For example, the generation of content may be executed by the crowd (case 1) or by an expert (case 2). It is therefore especially pertinent to analyze all crowdsourcing operations using this table as a framework.

---

4 By content, we mean a text, an idea, a video, an image, a sound, or any content liable to be transmitted by a network.

Crowdsourcing and Value Creation

The goal of every organization is to create value through its various activities. This remains true in the case of outsourcing. In this chapter, we will attempt to explain how a company can create value by means of a crowdsourcing operation. To do this, we will use a model linking types of value, types of crowd, and the means by which these crowds are accessed.

In classic outsourcing, it is possible to focus on the costs and on the notion of rare resources. From a cost perspective, we speak of transaction costs; the question is whether or not the cost of executing an activity internally is higher than the cost of the same activity when it is outsourced [WIL 85]. The first important point is that, seemingly in every case, crowdsourcing proves to be less expensive than other forms of outsourcing. This seems to us to be a crucial point, and it has not been sufficiently emphasized. However, even the very first example, given by J. Howe in 2006 [HOW 06] – the search for a photo by the National Health Museum – showed that the prices of istockphoto [1] (a case of crowdsourcing) were unbeatable when compared with those of a classic photographer (a case of outsourcing), even when the latter's prices were negotiable. The examples cited from Dell, Amazon, and Mechanical Turk also agree on the fact that crowdsourcing is cheap. However, the notion of price is not the only factor to be taken into account when outsourcing; there is also the notion of resources. This is known as resource-based theory

---

1 In the order of a few dollars.

[BAR 91]. The objective of this approach is to define an organization's resources and to outsource other activities. Crowdsourcing is fundamentally different on this point. Here the focus is not on resources; we presuppose that the crowd can contribute this resource. It is, then, a matter of implementing the means to capture this presupposed resource. Let us look first at the idea of value, and then at how it is possible to extract value from a relationship with a crowd.

3.1. Creation of value

The concept of value creation encompasses a wide range of indicators including competitiveness, performance, profitability, efficiency, effectiveness, satisfaction, and success. This wide spectrum illustrates the importance of the concept, but also reveals the absence of a true consensus on its definition. Thus, each disciplinary field has tended to develop from specific needs, approaches, and particular value-measurement instruments. This is the case, for example, with client satisfaction in the field of marketing, and with the value chain in the field of strategy [PAY 01]. In finance, creating value in the strictly financial and monetary sense is generally understood as creating value for shareholders in order to remunerate the risk taken, as funds proper are not a source of free financing. The creation of shareholder-centered value, or EVA (Economic Value Added) is also the central indicator for numerous business consultants or directors.

In our case, we will use the proposition made by Lefaix-Durant *et al.* [LEF 06], which consists of understanding value as a measurement of importance accorded by the particpants concerned; value creation therefore designates the process that restores to participants the assets they judge to be important. Certainly there is a link between value as a perception and value as a financial asset, but when studying the virtual social relation, we believe it is more relevant to focus first on this perception aspect.

Crowdsourcing falls within the domain of relationships diffused via information technology. In this context, an approach of value co-construction by the various participants has emerged [NOR 93], and numerous works have shown the specificity of electronic connections in value creation [AGU 07; KIM 09; MOL 07; AMI 01] estimating that, in the field of electronic business, value creation is based on four interconnected dimensions: efficiency, complementarity, lock-in, and novelty. This often-mentioned article[2] seems particularly pertinent in establishing a value-creation approach within the crowdsourcing context.

The figure below shows the four determinants of value-creation in the context of electronic relationships.

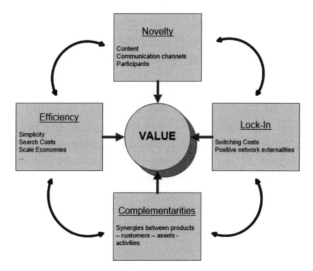

Figure 3.1. *Sources of value creation in e-business*
[AMI 01, p. 504]

Let us now explain these four determinants in order to illustrate how, and in what way, crowdsourcing can be a source of value:

– Novelty: innovation is a source of value. In electronic relationships, this applies to the intrinsic characteristics of the communication channel linking organizations and individuals; to the content of this relationship; and finally to the specific characteristics of the individuals involved in this type of relationship. More precisely,

---

2 Cited 103 times in articles available via sciencedirect, for example.

in electronic business, innovation is the result of the way in which business is done. Companies create value by connecting parties that were previously unconnected, by eliminating inefficiencies in the processes of purchase and sale, for example, by sensing the latent needs of consumers and/or creating entirely new markets.

– Efficiency: in a classic approach based on transaction costs, value is created when costs are minimized. These costs can be enumerated in terms of financial cost, speed of execution of an activity, or the simplicity limiting the cognitive effort involved in a task.

These two determining factors of value in the context of electronic relationships cover the range of motivations attached to the launch of a crowdsourcing operation. In fact, an empirical study has shown that the principal motives of business directors for crowdsourcing are: a) cost control and reduction, and the search for excellence and b) a large volume of opinions [LEB 08]. Moreover, it is this analysis of motives that has resulted in the conception of two types of crowdsourcing and, correlatively, two distinct ways of creating value. The first is that of crowdsourcing aimed at reducing the costs of routine activities that are non-strategic consumers of labor, a classic reason for outsourcing. The second is related to creative decision-making which leads to an emphasis on an original form of value creation in the domain of outsourcing.

– Complementarities: complementarity exists when a group of elements offers more value than the sum of the elements taken individually. This complementarity can exist between products and services, between "online" and "offline", between technologies, or between activities, for example. Virtual markets, which are characterized above all by strong interconnectivity, by the speed of information processes, and by the absence of geographical limitations, benefit greatly from these complementarities, which do not necessarily form at the heart of the relationship.

– Community lock-in: this is mainly a matter of creating value through the development of direct or indirect network externalities. These can be defined as follows: a product or technology obtains network externalities if its value for each user increases with the number of individuals who use it [BAN 09; UED 10]. K. Kelly

[KEL 98] showed this clearly by using the example of the fax, whose value increases with the number of people who use this means of communication. In this case, there is a positive externality that creates value. However, in other cases (congestion or saturation of the network), externalities can be negative and destructive of value.

These two other value determinants in the context of electronic relationships also have echoes in the crowdsourcing operations we have observed. In fact, some crowdsourcing operations seek complementarity above all, between the creation of videos meant for communication operations, the precise identification of the target for these same videos and their characteristics, and finally control of the real impact of the communications campaign executed with the help of these videos, for example. In terms of community affiliation and thus of the development of positive network externalities through crowdsourcing operations, this is manifested by developing the attractiveness of a crowdsourcing site in parallel to the number of Internet users who frequent it. For example, there is no immediate benefit for the participants in increasing the number of Internet users offering a video in response to a crowdsourcing operation.The opposite is actually true, since the degree of competition rises with the number of participants. However, increasing the number of participants indicates greater creative potential and may make crowdsourcing operations more attractive to organizations liable to outsource part of their communication in this way. Likewise, the participants will have the advantage of being more frequently solicited to participate in video competitions.

Value can thus be created through the electronic relationships at the heart of every crowdsourcing operation; likewise, the objective of any organization lies in the implementation of means to capture this value. It is therefore important for an organization to ensure its ability to capture the value created by a crowd of strangers within the context of virtual relationships. However, in order to be able to address this question, we must return to the type of value that a crowdsourcing operation can generate.

3.2. What type of value?

A crowdsourcing operation can create value through the following elements:

– Cost reduction. As indicated above, crowdsourcing is always less costly than a classic outsourcing operation. The question then becomes: why not systematically turn to crowdsourcing? As we will see in the next chapter, each crowdsourcing operation has a number of limitations that sometimes make it impossible to substitute it for outsourcing.

– Development of innovation that procures a competitive advantage against competitors and in this way contributes to creating value (that may be incremental or disruptive innovations).

– Authenticity, which consists of an organization's improved understanding of its environment, its market, or its clients. It allows a business to offer better-adapted products and services, and thus to create value.

The figure below summarizes these three sources of value creation.

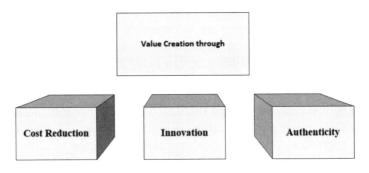

Figure 3.2. *Sources of value creation*

However, as we will see in the next section, while cost reduction is a constant, it becomes necessary to choose between innovation and authenticity, as these two objectives cannot coexist in a single crowdsourcing operation.

3.3. What type of crowd?

Our investigations have revealed that members of a crowd participate in crowdsourcing operations for two main reasons: passion and interest. Based on this, the crowd can be divided into two communities, which we will call: a) the "passionate-skilled" community and b) the "skilled-passionate" community, to account for the priorities characterizing each of them. Also note that these two communities are not airtight, but rather constitute the two extremes at either side of a continuum, in the center of which a hybrid community resides. This hybrid community includes individuals who have an average skill level and a limited passion for the task. We note that these two elements can contribute to reducing the interest this crowd might possess; indeed, when our passion is lukewarm we spend less time on a task, and if on top of this the skill is not there to compensate for this limited attention span, the value added by this type of crowd is at risk of being relatively low.

Let us take a more detailed look at the two types of crowd we have distinguished, which prove to be based on their respective motivations. For this reason, in order to analyze them and their motivations and to go beyond the specific motivations used for each of them, we have chosen to focus on the work of psychologists on this subject [DEC 87].

The "passionate-skilled" community [PC]

This type of community is characterized by the "fervent" attention it brings to a task; a very high level of interest in a specific task frequently connected to a product brand (improving a product) or a service brand (conducting investigative journalism for the benefit of a highly-reputed newspaper). We have observed that the motivation of members of this type of community is focused on an individual desire to improve the center of interest that brings them together. Moreover, they are not usually paid for their participation. In this case it is the task itself and not the task as a means to an end that above all motivates this community. This type of crowd is therefore driven by intrinsic motivations, as shown in the table below.

Characteristics of intrinsic motivation	Nature of skills	Level and range of skills
The beauty of the gesture; altruistic overall. Belonging to a community; a network as a goal in itself.	Focused on a task linked to a brand and/or product or service attached to it.	Variable level but limited range.

Table 3.1. *Characteristics of the passionate-skilled community*

How, then, do we enter into a relationship with this type of crowd, and stimulate its participation? Since intrinsic motivations are linked to the task concerning, in the case of crowdsourcing, a brand and/or the product or service attached to it, this brand must be attractive enough to possess a large enough community made up mostly of consumers. Ethical behavior towards its community on the part of the organization using crowdsourcing, as well as with regard to "trendy" values such as sustainable development and ecology are also important. It is highly probable that within the crowd "watchdogs" will exist, who are always ready to denounce what might be perceived as a betrayal of the community. If they feel betrayed, members of the community may no longer be able to identify themselves with the brand, which will lead to a rapid dissolution of the community.[3] The use of techniques favoring consumer immersion in order to reinforce the connection between brand and consumers, as recommended in experiential marketing approaches, is also adapted for this case. This is manifested particularly in website support of the crowdsourcing operation, notably its level of user-friendliness.

Finally, the participation of passionate consumers will be strengthened by their promotion within the community, which consists of showing Internet users that their ideas will truly be taken into account and – the highest point of pride – will then be integrated into forthcoming products. The strong sentiment of "shared paternity" of the product, along with the feeling of belonging to a community or network, can only attract followers.

---

3 The polemic against the use of noxious products by the "eco-friendly" brand Ushuaïa is a good example of this.

The "skilled-passionate" community [CP]

It is undeniable that the members of this type of community are seeking, above all, the satisfaction of material interest – mainly in the form of financial remuneration. In this case, it is the external environment of the task that motivates an Internet user more than anything else. The task is a means and not an end; the behavior of this type of crowd is therefore governed by extrinsic motivations.

The community assembles and then unites around the business model proposed by the organization holding the crowdsourcing operation. The table below describes the characteristics of this type of community.

Characteristics of extrinsic motivation	Nature of skills	Level of skills
Financial remuneration.	Focused on the demands of the party holding the activity.	Variable but tending toward high.

Table 3.2. *Characteristics of the skilled-passionate community*

What are the incentives that attract this type of crowd?

We will put forward a threefold idea here. First, with regard to the site itself, it is advisable for the organization managing the crowdsourcing operation to propose a pertinent and coherent business model that will guarantee that the Internet user does not suffer any harm. From this perspective, questions of intellectual property rights and discoverer remuneration are essential [AYE 10]. An idea must never be appropriated without remunerating its creator. Unfortunately, we meet entrepreneurs all too often who would like to make use of a skilled crowd to help them resolve their problems, but who do not wish to pay for it.

Secondly, the site supporting the crowdsourcing must be respectable and credible. Contracts signed with well-known clients, for example, will contribute to this respectability. Thirdly, payments made directly to "finders" are exclusively financial in nature. These may be fees determined in advance; high and clearly stated amounts, which also reinforce the credibility of the site. On the other hand, it is important to note that the success factors associated with the SP community are no longer in their infancy. Thus, a discoverer may be more concerned with the material benefit he/she may receive from the effective implementation of his/her idea than by pride of authorship.

Hybrid community

This includes people who do not participate in crowdsourcing operations due to pure passion for a brand or the product/service associated with it; however, they are not driven by financial remuneration alone, either. This type of crowd can be highly volatile and its contributions extremely variable. Contributors to the *Istockphoto* website, for example, can be placed in this category. Their motivations are certainly linked initially to financial remuneration, but throughout the course of their participation, these motivations evolve toward belonging to a community and the opportunities that go along with it, particularly in terms of visibility. In this case, we are dealing with internalized extrinsic motivations.

The table below describes this hybrid community.

Characteristics of internalized extrinsic motivation	Nature of skills	Level of skills	Examples
Status, visibility, opportunities.	Focused on the task and what can be derived from it.	Variable/average.	- Istockphoto. - France 24 observers. - Nokia calling all innovators.

Table 3.3. *Characteristics of the hybrid community*

How, then, do we motivate this type of crowd? We do this by offering the possibility of finding better employment in the future, or simply by flattering the crowd's ego. However, the ambiguous character of this community's motivations also suggests the use of stimuli proper to the two other communities, but with variable intensity. For example, the payment offered for a given task will generally be lower.

To conclude, in order to grasp the potential value of a crowd we must determine the type of crowd fulfilling the expectations for the crowdsourcing operation concerned. Only then can we match the type of crowd to the specific motivations that work best with it, in the following manner:

– Passionate-skilled: reacts to intrinsic motivations; that is, motivations connected to the task.

– Skilled-passionate: reacts to extrinsic motivations; that is, financial motivations.

– Hybrid: reacts to internalized extrinsic motivations; that is, motivations connected to individual status and visibility.

We would add that the mixed character of internalized extrinsic motivations allows them to be used to stimulate the two other types of crowd.

Now let us determine the links liable to exist between the type of crowd and the forms of value sought in a crowdsourcing operation.

The table below summarizes our remarks and illustrates the links between the type of crowd and form of value sought.

		Form of value sought	
		Authenticity	Innovation
Types of crowd	Skilled-passionate	Difficult to define, since the solutions offered are linked to the expected benefit (financial remuneration) and not to the brand, product, or service.	Creation of value through conceptual and cognitive diversity. Skills and distance facilitate the creation of innovations. Selected by the business.
	Passionate-skilled	Creation of value via the proximity between crowd, brand, and product or service. Emergence of a dominant feeling. Selected by the crowd.	Low diversity of skills reduces the probability of an occurrence of innovation.

Table 3.4. *Links between type of crowd and form of value sought*

Finally, let us look at the case of a hybrid crowd. This type of crowd is driven by internalized extrinsic motivations and reacts in particular to motivations that increase the visibility of members within the community and offer professional opportunities. At this stage of our investigations, we believe this type of crowd can suggest improvements to existing products. However, the remoteness of the crowd and of the product can lead to a situation in which these improvements are not shared by the product's community of consumers. Thus, these will not be radical innovations or authentic creations.

Now that we have discussed the concept of value and the types of crowd, we will look at how all of these elements can be grouped coherently in an adapted business model.

3.4. Towards an adapted business model

We believe it is important for every entrepreneur to have a clear idea, at a given time t, of his/her company's business model. There are many definitions of this term, as well as methodologies aimed at facilitating its construction. We will refer here to the famous model created by Osterwalder and Pigneur [OST 10], since its authors have a perfect understanding of the issues related to organizations and technologies, as well as a solid academic foundation, which has allowed them to propose a method that is scientifically rigorous while directly addressing the practical issues faced by entrepreneurs.

However, prior to the construction of any business model we are faced with the idea that if this model involves the use of crowdsourcing, it must distinguish two categories of tasks: those undertaken internally and those entrusted to the crowd.

In further exploration of this idea, the next chapter will offer a large number of variations on the crowdsourcing concept, which many entrepreneurs may find of use.

First, let us consider the division of tasks between internal resources and the crowd. Currently, a crowdsourcing operation can be used to carry out two major types of task: content generation (ideas, texts, videos, etc.) and content selection (identifying good ideas from within the content generated). The crowd is not necessarily involved in all these tasks, as shown in the figure below.

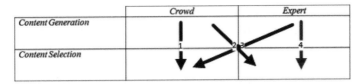

	Crowd	Expert
Content Generation		
Content Selection		

Figure 3.3. *Tasks and choice between crowd and expert*

Arrow 1: activity in which the crowd undertakes the tasks of content generation and selection.

Arrow 2: activity in which the crowd suggests content, but in which a group of experts subsequently selects the content that best corresponds to the expectations of the company that initiated the crowdsourcing operation.

Arrow 3: activity in which experts suggest content that will then be selected by the crowd via a voting system, for example. In this case it is the crowd that identifies the content judged to be pertinent and the content which is not.

Arrow 4: activity that does not utilize the crowd and thus cannot be considered a crowdsourcing operation.

Once tasks devolve to the specified crowd, it is important to connect the crowd to the company's objectives in using crowdsourcing.

Though there are many forms of crowdsourcing, as we will see in the following chapter, the nature of the tasks that may be entrusted to the crowd can be of only two types: simple or complex [GUI 10; GUI 11]. If the task to be carried out is simple (meaning that it is possible to put routines into practice to complete it), the source of value creation is mainly financial. It is a simple matter of making a calculation, as we will see in the case of crowdjobbing later on. But if the task is complex, the entrepreneur must identify his/her objective when he/she turns to crowdsourcing, as well as the type of crowd that will allow him/her to achieve this objective.

One of the principal results of our research was to show that, for complex tasks, entrepreneurs must choose whether they are seeking authenticity or innovation from the crowd (we will explain these terms later). This is because the types of crowds to be mobilized for each case differ; a crowd should be made up of passionate individuals if authenticity is sought, and made up of skilled individuals if innovation is sought. The stimuli to be used are also specific to each of the two types of crowd; the key to success in a crowdsourcing operation for a complex task lies in balancing the proper motivation with the objective sought in the use of the crowd.

The figure below summarizes these results of our research.

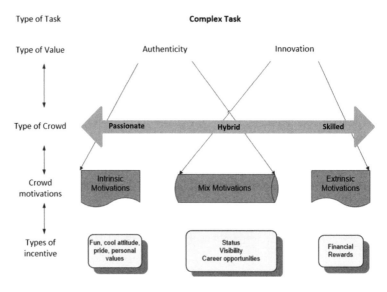

Figure 3.4. *Connecting crowd and company objectives*

As an illustration, we will now give some examples that will be more broadly developed in the next chapter. A business is seeking innovative answers to its problems through the use of crowdsourcing. Depending on its objective, it must call on skilled individuals coming from disciplines that are sometimes extremely unlike those normally used. These people will respond to the challenge proposed by the business, not because they like this company or because they are passionate about the question posed, but because responding will bring them something. Their motivation is extrinsic. Thus, the company, in order to attract this crowd, must offer motivation that is mainly financial; and moreover, the more the financial compensation that is offered, the more it will increase the number of people tempted to take on the challenge, as well as the probability of obtaining an appropriate response to the question posed.

Conversely, let us look at the case of a business seeking to know the deep feelings of a crowd for its products. If it offers financial motivation, it will attract individuals who are interested not in its products but rather in the money they might earn. Thus, this type of stimulus will not gain the company true knowledge of these deep feelings. Rather, for this they will have to offer motivations directly linked to its products (create a limited, personalized series of the product for the winner, for example). This type of motivation will only interest people who are really passionate about the products, and the ideas and feelings expressed will be truly authentic.

Of course, there is a continuum between innovation and authenticity, and between extrinsic and intrinsic motivation. It is therefore possible to have a crowd whose motivations are hybrid (semi-passionate and semi-skilled), who is interested in the product but also desires financial compensation related to the accomplishment of the task. Calling on this type of crowd leads to a slight loss of innovation or authenticity, but it also leads to a gain in volume. In short, it is always a question of dosage. The proper motivations must be defined in order to bring out a community whose characteristics will help the business to attain its objective is a field of research that must continue to be explored. For example, sensitivity studies linking the amount of motivation to the number and quality of responses obtained are worthy of being conducted.

Once the objectives and motivations have been defined we can move on to the final stage: the definition of the business model.

Remember that crowdsourcing is an operation in which a task is outsourced to a crowd. Here, we will place ourselves alongside a business using crowdsourcing, and not one for which crowdsourcing is the core of the business model – that is, a business selling crowdsourcing as a service, such as Innocentive, for example.

Thus, for a business that turns to crowdsourcing, we will focus on the cost portion of Osterwalder and Pigneur's framework. Indeed, we would prefer not to speak of return on investment (ROI), since in the majority of cases, discussions of ROI are scattered and impossible to define (see Solow's famous paradox).

The figure below shows the positions of the contributions and questions raised for a business model by a crowdsourcing operation.

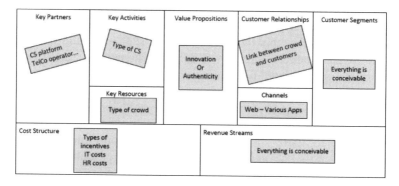

Figure 3.5. *BM framework*

Let us look back briefly at these cases.

For key partners, it will be necessary to determine which platform will support the crowdsourcing operation. This may be an external service provider specializing in crowdsourcing, or simply an IT supplier that will support the traffic caused by this outsourcing.

The key activities to be outsourced will be discussed in the next chapter.

The key resources are constituted by the crowd, and more precisely by a certain type of crowd (from passionate to skilled).

Value will be created in terms of innovation or authenticity.[4]

The structure of costs must take into account the motivations used to attract the crowd. This cost structure includes mainly the costs of information technology and human capital (a community manager, for example).

Finally, though we have focused on the left-hand side of the framework, we must mention the "client relations" block. Indeed, we must never forget that the crowd participating in a crowdsourcing operation is also made up of business clients.

The concept of crowdsourcing has been in existence for seven years, and we have chosen to provide frameworks and grids for explanatory purposes before presenting categories and examples.

The next chapter will discuss current variations of crowdsourcing.

---

4 We will not discuss the outsourcing of a simple and routine task here; in this case, value is created in terms of cost reduction and time gain.

4

Forms of Crowdsourcing

Crowdsourcing may be understood as a generic way to use a crowd for an outsourcing operation. The objective of this section is to examine in detail the various forms crowdsourcing may take, by presenting and discussing ten types of crowdsourcing operation.

As we have seen, the crowd offers many potentialities:

– ongoing presence;

– availability;

– speedy reaction.

In addition, the crowd can be seen as a resource that is abundant, cheap, and motivated all at once.

In the introduction to this chapter, we will briefly answer the following three questions:

– Which tasks cannot be outsourced to crowdsourcing?

– Which tasks can only be outsourced to crowdsourcing?

– Which tasks cannot be outsourced at all?

These types of question are very often raised when this kind of intervention is discussed with managers.

Let us begin with the last question. Can everything be outsourced? Proponents of the resource theory described above would say no. A business cannot outsource any rare resources it possesses. Managers do not believe strategy can be outsourced. Yet, what is the job of a strategy consultant, if not to carry out part of the strategic activity that could be executed internally? From our perspective and in our experience, all activities can be outsourced. However, this does not mean that businesses will all become nothing but contractual connectors and disappear. Even though we can find examples of outsourcing for the vast majority of tasks executed by organizations, the outsourcing approach is not unproblematic.

This leads us to the first question: which tasks cannot be outsourced to crowdsourcing? Here, we can respond that crowdsourcing requires establishing a close relationship with the crowd. To do this, the technological media is necessary. Therefore, any tasks that cannot be routed through this media will not involve crowdsourcing. For example, the negotiation of an important contract, which requires face-to-face meetings and meals in good restaurants, cannot be the subject of a crowdsourcing operation.

Finally, we turn to the most difficult question: which tasks can only be outsourced to crowdsourcing? We have asked ourselves this question thousands of times, and come to the conclusion that it is not relevant. In fact, we have not found a single task that can only be carried out by a crowd of anonymous individuals. However, we have noted that many businesses do not use crowdsourcing to outsource tasks that they have always done internally in the past; rather, they initiate new activities directly via crowdsourcing operations. Thus, crowdsourcing allows businesses to undertake tasks they could not have executed before. The proper question to ask becomes, then: what new activities can businesses undertake thanks to crowdsourcing?

The ten types of crowdsourcing shown below provide an emphatic answer to this question.

4.1. Crowdjobbing

Outsourced activity	Multiple varying routine tasks or a single and very specific task.
Characteristics of outsourced activity	The principal task must be able to be broken down and then reassembled once the sub-tasks are completed. It must be possible to control the quality of the finished work. The principal task is not directly strategic, though the use of the final result can be of strategic interest. The cost of automating this task must be higher than the cost of outsourcing it.
Secondary effects	The work of some ill-qualified people in the company may be called into question. The work of certain specialists such as linguists may be affected.
Future of this method	This solution may appeal greatly to enlightened bureaucracies; meaning organizations confronted with administrative tasks with little added value but which desire to be efficient nonetheless. The cleaning of Big Data may also be suited to this type of outsourcing.
Some examples	BusinessLeads – https://businessleads.com/ Click Worker – http://www.clickworker.com/en/ CloudCrowd – http://www.cloudcrowd.com MechanicalTurk – https://www.mturk.com/ Servio – http://www.serv.io/

Table 4.1. *Summary of crowdjobbing*

4.1.1. *What is it?*

This is one of the oldest forms of crowdsourcing. In fact, J. Howe cited it in his seminal article [HOW 06]. He did not yet use this term, but described "Mechanical Turk", a solution offered by Amazon, the stated goal of which was to create a labor market.[1] Its mode of functioning is relatively simple and tremendously effective. It is a meeting place for those offering work and those seeking jobs. The companies advertising work are characterized by offering projects that can be broken down into simple tasks; these projects, then, are complicated but not complex. Remember that, by definition, a complex task cannot be broken down into simpler ones. From the perspective of the job advertisers, these jobs will be taken by individuals who are anonymous and content to do work that is easy and low-paid.

The world of translation may also be impacted upon. Imagine the difficulty for translation software of translating text-speak from one language to another.

As effectively shown by Kittur *et al.* [KIT 13] (see Figure 4.1), this method of crowdsourcing affects the entire labor market.

However, crowdjobbing can also include the execution of unique and very specific tasks, as we will see with Businessleads. In this case, a seller seeks buyers for its products. It will use Businessleads to instruct the crowd to bring clients to it. This is a specific and unique request:

> "I am looking for a person who will put me in contact with buyers for my flagship product. Of course, this middleman will be paid."

This payment is called a "bounty".

---

1 Marketplace for work.

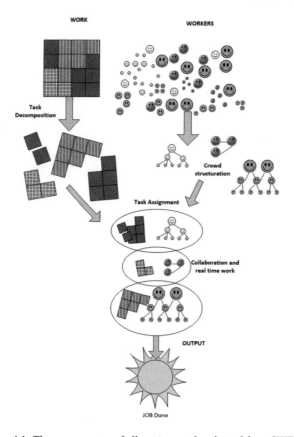

Figure 4.1. *The new process of allocating work, adapted from [KIT 13]*

4.1.2. *Why it works*

Crowdjobbing is of interest because it offers:

– a speedy access to a workforce;

– a high volume of available labor and a wide variety of potentially-interested individuals;

– a permanently available workforce;

– the fact that payment is made by the commissioning party only once the task has been completed;

– people all over the world who are ready to work for sums that may seem low to Westerners.

Given these conditions, this type of outsourcing cannot fail to work.

4.1.3. *Limitations*

The first limitation is ethical. There are barriers against remote use and without verification of a low-cost work force. It is impossible to know if a child might or might not be behind the computer. Without entering into a debate on the concept of ethics, the danger for a company is that a report showing this kind of outsourcing as a new type of exploitation might be broadcast. It is therefore a matter of great delicacy for the business to provide justification for its professional actions.

The second limitation is related to the type of task that can be involved. In the first place, this task must be able to broken down into smaller tasks, which is not always the case. Generating opinions on books, for example, cannot be done by cutting a 300-page book into 600 half-pages and then distributing these. Secondly, crowdjobbing can currently be used only for virtual tasks, though this fact may change in the future. We might imagine that the sending of a parcel from point A to point B can be broken down into x sub-journeys and that one person would transport the parcel on each of these sections. Thirdly, the costs of breakdown/reassembly and verification add to the payments that must be made for the work carried out by the crowd, and the overall sum of these costs must be less than the cost of processing the task internally.

$$Sc + Rc + Cc + WLc + PF \leq Ic$$

Sc: splitting cost;

Rc: reassembling cost;

Cc: checking cost;

WLc: work/labor cost;

PF: platform fee;

Ic: internal cost.

The two variables are the costs of breakdown and reassembly: this implies that the task will be well-managed via computers. For example, in the case of a geographical map, georeferencing data and various strata of information (population, habitations, etc.) must be correctly stored in manipulable databases.

The verification variable can be integrated into the sub-tasks to be carried out. In fact, just as when we were in school and sometimes corrected the work of a classmate, we might imagine that all or part of the sub-tasks will be carried out two or more times. We can also imagine that verification might be done internally on test samples.

The price variable of the sub-task can also vary. According to the law of supply and demand, if the price is too low, there will be few candidates to carry out the sub-tasks, and the higher the price the faster the task is completed. This is, then, an important variable.

Nevertheless, cost is not a neutral factor, and as we know in accounting control, it is quite difficult to determine internal costs.

4.1.4. *The future*

The earliest cases of crowdjobbing were concentrated on the "demand" part of the labor market, i.e. companies proposed their services to carry out tasks. Now, and as shown by Fiverr, the "offer" aspect on the part of the crowd is beginning to emerge. Individuals propose to carry out tasks for sums beginning as low as $5.00, and clients emerge from the crowd to purchase these services. Here we see what used to be found in newspapers or on the street, when a person offered his/her services to repair a chair, for example, or to sharpen a knife.

Crowdjobbing can be used for both virtual and physical tasks.

Let us look at these two types of possibilities.

With regard to virtual tasks, we must keep in mind that crowdjobbing concerns large ensembles that can be broken down. In this context, the concept of Big Data seems particularly appropriate. Two problems can then be solved by crowdjobbing.

Firstly, the cleaning-up of data constitutes an essential task that is very dull and possesses little intrinsic added value.

The task of data clean-up can be subdivided into two distinct tasks: detecting problems and carrying out the data repair operation.

In a large data mass there can be missing data, incomplete data, erroneous data, incorrectly-formatted data (capital letters instead of lowercase ones, for example), and incorrectly-referenced data. In the past, "useless data" would have been added to this list. However, with current storage capacities, it is sensible to keep as much data as possible and to throw only very little of it away. Thus, the first sub-activity in clean-up consists of detecting these flaws within the data mass. With large volumes and a constant supply of new data, it can be interesting to separate stored data from the flow adding to it and to give the stores to a crowd of "processors".

The second sub-activity is to clean or repair data flagged up as problematic. This task can be carried out by the same crowd as the previous task, or by another crowd with different skills.

We now turn to physical tasks. A site such as TaskRabbit.com is an example of this. The act of calling on a person to carry out a task such as "assemble a piece of IKEA furniture" shows this continuity between the virtual world (a person requests help and offers a price to carry out a task via a website) and the physical world (an Internet user goes to the person's home and concretely assembles this piece of furniture). But this already exists; let us look a little more closely.

Any small local production can be mobilized in order to ensure a targeted micro-distribution. Imagine, for example, a publicity campaign aimed at small businesses in a rural area. The advertising material may be a printout that can be generated by any color printer using a pre-made template to which the Internet user adds only the store name. Each Internet user is paid per store. In a short time, a campaign can be launched nationwide and even reach areas that are obscure and not necessarily referenced in databases.

In the case of the use of 3D printers, the potential increases exponentially. It may be possible to send design models of small advertising objects that Internet users would then print and distribute. The details of controlling this process remain to be defined, but it would be a way to have a mass of distributors who could be rapidly mobilized in a given geographical area.

4.2. Crowdwisdom

Outsourced activity	Seeking answers to questions.
Characteristics of outsourced activity	The question must be able to be formalized in a way that is simple and accessible to as many people as possible.
Secondary effects	Survey bureaus may be consulted less often.
Future of this method	Easy to implement and powerful; this method will continue to develop.
Some examples	Vote Online for Miss Universe[2]: any site that creates and moderates a discussion forum where clients can post their problems and others can respond to them. Lulu: a site where authors can publish and sell their books. Of course, some books are generated from this. Threadless: a very well-known site to commission and sell t-shirts with logos. CafePress: the same type of site, selling mugs as well.

Table 4.2. *Crowdwisdom summary table*

---

2 http://www.missuniverse.com/missu2012voting/faq.html.

4.2.1. *What is it?*

Outsourced activity: opinions and thoughts on a subject

Traditional supplier: experts, critics, and "opinion-makers".

One of the fundamental tenets of democracy lies in the belief that if a large enough number of people hold a certain opinion, they are right. A country like Switzerland, in which the use of referendums is frequent and which is considered an example of democracy, illustrates this view.

The concept of crowdwisdom is therefore to apply the referendum concept to all kinds of subjects.

4.2.2. *Why it works*

Calling on the opinion of the crowd is not really anything new. The key factor here is the possibility of being able to give a "grade" in order to give weight to one's opinion, and/or to give an opinion on the thinking of others.

Let us take a more detailed look at these two mechanisms. The first one consists of linking a qualitative opinion to a quantitative indicator. The choice can be to assign a certain number of stars, as in rating products on Amazon, for example. In anonymous academic peer review processes, the evaluator is asked to indicate his/her level of expertise on the subject. For example, in the easychair[3] platform, the evaluator must choose from among five categories ranging from none to expert. This weighting helps the person analyzing the responses. The second mechanism consists of the simple but powerful choice between "I like it" and "I don't like it". This mechanism can constitute a crowdwisdom operation all by itself. The magic of this function lies in the fact that opinions or ideas emerge from or disappear into the ether in such an automatic way.

---

3 http://www.easychair.org/.

4.2.3. *Limitations*

When J. Howe cited the example of the game show "Who Wants to be a Millionaire?" and its "Ask the Audience" lifeline, he stipulated that only people who knew the answer tended to respond. In fact, in this game we do not normally see an intention to damage the contestant's chances for success. But the Internet does not always work like this, and there are many reasons for people to have bad intentions: economic competition, political differences, etc. It is therefore quite possible that an opinion will be expressed "just to be harmful" and to use levers to multiply this vote (calling on a particular group or even paying people to vote).

A few years before his death, the writer Volkoff [VOL 02] brought to light two major mechanisms that possess limits but which delineate society's choices: the democratic mechanism, based on a quantitative approach, and the aristocratic mechanism, based according to him on a qualitative approach. Still according to this author, the functioning of democracy is only improved if it is combined with a dose of quantitative input, and thus of skill. Moreover, the total democratization of the Internet has led to the generation of unprecedented numbers of people offering their opinion on anything and everything. Without being too critical of the musical talents of the singer Psy, we will simply note that as of early April 2013 his famous video "Gangnam Style" had been viewed more than 1.5 billion times in 9 months. By way of comparison, Mozart has not exceeded 30 million views in 4 years and Beethoven can boast 60 million – due largely to a Justin Bieber video called "Justin Bieber vs. Beethoven". In short, the question of the respondents' competency on subjects requiring some reflection may be asked with justification.

4.2.4. *The future*

Two paths can be foreseen. The first is that of generalization. The ease of giving one's opinion (a short text or even just a click) allows this mechanism to be massively diffused via any type of device (smartphone, tablets, Google Glass, etc.). We must wait to see whether this type of outsourcing will become obligatory for any participant needing an opinion. The second path is the niche market path. Some subjects require a certain level of expertise. It may be possible to implement a selective process of bestowing permission to vote. However, this selection mechanism must be based on the seeking of skills and not the simple collection of information for business purposes. Some sites, for example, do not allow the posting of opinions unless a person is subscribed to the website in question. This mechanism does not take into account the user's skill, and therefore in no way prejudices his/her capacity to offer a relevant opinion. It simply indicates the user's motivation.

4.3. Crowdfunding

Outsourced activity	Financing.
Type of projects concerned	Projects requiring a low or moderate amount of investment. Any project that can be publicly presented can be involved.
Secondary effects	Traditional financing networks can be impacted and hold up or try to include this method in their offer.
Future of this method	Very promising.
Some examples	Kickstarter – Mymajorcompany – Ulule – kisskissbangbang.

Table 4.3. *Summary of crowdfunding*

4.3.1. *What is it?*

Crowdfunding can be defined as a resource allowing a project initiator to obtain financing from Internet users. This financing can involve all or part of the initiator's capital needs. Even though there is nothing to prevent any project initiator from dedicating a part of his/her website to financing, we have observed that crowdfunding is supported by specialized platforms. There are three participants: first, the individuals or businesses proposing a project. These projects may be new and innovative ideas, and financial resources are necessary to develop them. They may also be existing businesses seeking to diversify and which may use this method to test the pertinence of their ideas with the public. The second participating entity is made up of

Internet users wishing to participate in the proposed venture. As we will see in this method's reasons for success, the motivations of Internet users vary but overall their interest is not only financial. Finally, the third participant is located at the interface between project initiators and the crowd. These are the platforms that put the two other participants in contact with each other. They offer:

– An easy-to-access place where the crowd may look at potential projects.

– A guarantee of seriousness in the processing of financial flow.

– Occasional expertise in the ergonomics of project presentation (structure, formatting).

Regarding the business model of crowdfunding, in general the platform earns from 5% to 8% of the total amount of the funded project. In the case of an unfunded project, the crowd earns back its investment minus approximately 2%. Thus, the platform is always earning money even if it cannot truly be considered "big money".

4.3.2. An illustrative example

We will now look in more detail at the case of the documentary film entitled *Inocente*, which took place from 2012 to 2013.

Figure 4.2. *Documentary and crowdfunding project*

On February 24, 2013, the famous Academy Awards ceremony boasted its usual surprises, but we found one of the winners particularly interesting. In the documentary film category, Sean Fine and Andrea Nix Fine won an Oscar in the category "Best Short Documentary Film". The originality stemmed not only from the quality of this film, but also from the way in which it had been financed: crowdfunding. 294 Internet users had contributed $52,574 via the participatory financing platform Kickstarter. What should we note about this?

Firstly, it is certainly not the only film financed in this way to have been nominated (*King's Point* is another example), nor is it the first time such films have been financed in this way, but this is the first Academy Award.

Next, the average amount donated by each Internet user is fairly low; $180 on average, with more than 95% of Internet donors investing less than $250. The breakdown of these amounts is somewhat interesting, as shown in the figure below.

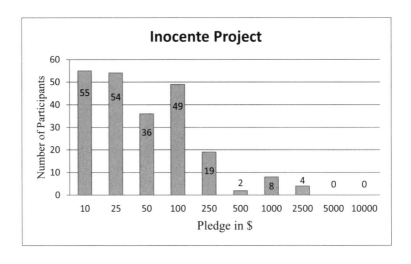

Figure 4.3. *Number of participants and amount invested*

Finally, a heightened buzz for this type of film has rapidly developed, since the short film has generated as many searches as the documentary (film category) that won the Oscar, while in general these kinds of productions are talked about far less often[4].

The second example we will now discuss also shows the limitations of this kind of financing. The project was for a "Food Truck"; that is, a traveling truck offering food cooked on the spot. The environment was highly favorable: in the US the same sort of projects have been launched; in France there are a few food trucks mostly dedicated to burgers, and finally, it is notable that the project began without experience or brand notoriety. The "Kluger Pies" brand had already existed for several years, and still possesses a shop and kitchen in which excellent pies are baked and sold. There have also been varied events held on site and the media coverage of these was very good. Numerous newspapers have cited the brand. Moreover, the inventor has published a cookbook that sold more than 100,000 copies. In addition, the Food Truck concept is currently quite trendy; a simple search for this term in Google returned almost 8 million results. Finally, the website chosen for the online financing proposal is the best-known site of this domain in France: "MyMajorCompany" (MMC). Yet, unfortunately, after 3 months of waiting, the €30,000 requested for starting up the food truck project has not been obtained. This case has surprised us, as all the proper indicators seemed to be in place. This raises several questions: was this platform relevant? Was the reward offered (€10 to begin) high enough? We can learn from this example that the answers to these questions are not obvious and that crowdfunding requires a great deal of further study.

4.3.3. *Why it works*

From our perspective, besides the novelty aspect, three factors lead to the success of this method: proximity to the project being financed, the taste for gambling, and a certain convenience.

---

4 A search for "inocente" "Sean Fine" "Andrea Nix Fine" yielded 200,000 results on Google and 33,800 on Bing, and the search "Searching for Sugar man" "Malik Bendjelloul" "Simon Chinn" yielded 236,000 results on Google and 35,900 on Bing (search conducted on February 26, 2013).

Firstly, we believe the proximity aspect is very important. As with the authenticity aspect, which we will see later on, financers all have a bond with the project. Thus, crowdsourcing projects generally include a dose of proximity, or closeness, with their public. Whether a proximity of ideas (as in some ethical or artistic projects) or a geographical proximity (as in projects concerning a site near their target public), these two elements are the glue in a relationship in which one person helps another by means of a minor virtual effort (a wire transfer from one account to another).

Proximity can also take a surprising form: the role of the fame of the party initiating the project. It is clear that projects proposed by well-known individuals are successful and widely financed. From our perspective, this is due to the fact that fame can be seen as a kind of bond of proximity between a person and a crowd.

The second success factor is related to a certain taste for gambling. The MMC site was one of the first to offer participants motivations in the form of bets.

This involved the financing of a play starring two well-known French actors, Claude Brasseur and Patrick Chesnais. MMC offered rewards for participation that varied depending on how many seats were filled in the auditorium.

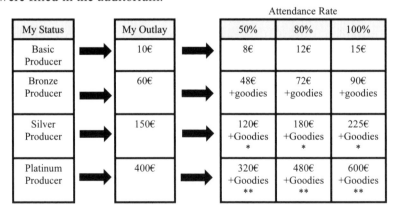

			Attendance Rate		
My Status	My Outlay		50%	80%	100%
Basic Producer	10€		8€	12€	15€
Bronze Producer	60€		48€ +goodies	72€ +goodies	90€ +goodies
Silver Producer	150€		120€ +Goodies *	180€ +Goodies *	225€ +Goodies *
Platinum Producer	400€		320€ +Goodies **	480€ +Goodies **	600€ +Goodies **

Figure 4.4. *Motivations in the form of bets (taken from the original table on the MyMajorCompany website)*

What can we note from this?

With regard to probability of gains, if we apply a probability of 33% to each rate, we get the probabilities of gain given in the following table.

Stake	Mathematical probability of gain	ROI in percentage
10	€1.7	16.7%
60	€10.0	16.7%
150	€25.0	16.7%
400	€66.7	16.7%

Table 4.4. *Probability of gains*

"Convenience: money" is a very specific concept. It is a mediator globally understood by everyone. It is also very well-suited for an Internet user who does not have a lot of time; he/she can simply read a project summary and make an electronic payment, with the whole transaction taking only 15 minutes.

There is another, final factor about which we remain somewhat dubious: return on investment. We are doubtful for two reasons; one is that, in following the financing curves of projects with and without a return on investment, we have not noted any significant correlation with the success or failure of the project. The second reason is that the vast majority of sums invested by Internet users are low (less than €100). These days, a return on investment of 10% is very high in the Western world, but a 10% return on €100 is only €10, which seems too low to motivate most people.

4.3.4. *Limitations*

Crowdfunding currently lies in a gray area of fiscal regulation. In France, crowdfunding may be compared to a Public Call for Savings, but in the United States it is difficult to use shares as remuneration [STE 13].

This method is not currently used for large projects. Although, some projects have brought a return of nearly one million dollars[5], most of them fall below €30,000.

4.3.5. *The future*

The near future will position crowdsourcing as a mandatory stage for every new business attempting to launch. Indeed, capital contributors are asking young entrepreneurs more and more often to test themselves on a crowdfunding platform. For them, this is a reliable indicator of the success or failure of an idea. If a community has financed an idea, this means that there is a seed present that is ready and able to grow into a thriving plant.

The future will also involve what we call "glocal" innovations; that is, a product that involves a large number of people on the global level but which can be individually accessed by everyone. The question will be, "can this kind of innovation be launched by an unknown entity, or must it be supported by a respected company?". The example of the documentary cited above gives us reason to believe that the unknowns have a chance. It seems certain, however, that large brands will use this method to test and develop their products. The risk is that Internet users may not feel the necessity of helping a Sony, for example. The marketing design of the project will be essential for bringing into play the idea of shared experience and common adventure.

Another point that may concern the future of crowdfunding is the financing of humanitarian projects. Currently, there is a certain amount of competitiveness between projects and a few economies of scale in the call on crowds for financing. Each organization makes its calls individually and often without having sufficient media coverage. There is an opportunity here for a humanitarian "kickstarter" who would bring together the calls. Moreover, this method works very well for one-time emergency appeals. For example, an earthquake in Iran or an oil spill in the Gulf of Mexico, or a drought with devastating effects on the population of Kenya, are all projects necessitating an urgent call and are limited regarding time-frame.

---

5 http://www.kickstarter.com/projects/syrp/genie-motion-control-time-lapse-device.

4.4. Crowdsourcing and forecasting

Outsourced activity	Expectation
Characteristics of outsourced activity	Limited and known number of potential solutions. High-visibility activity containing powerful controversies.
Secondary effects	Tradition survey institutes and traditional decision-makers may feel threatened in their prerogatives.
Future of this method	Small-scale solution but one that should endure.
Some examples	Qmarket – Inkling

Table 4.5. *"Crowd for Prediction" summary table*

4.4.1. *What is it?*

The use of the crowd to plan or predict is a way of outsourcing the classic survey activity usually entrusted to specialized institutes. We can also see, in this method of crowdsourcing, decision-making assistance based on the participation of a community of members. Gaspoz [GAS 11] shows, for example, how this method can be used to select from a portfolio of R&D projects, the one that members find the most promising. The principle is fairly simple and echoes that of a classic financial market. There are a certain number of products to be exchanged (the various alternatives) and, at the beginning, a price for each of them (this can begin from an identical price for each value). Participants have a certain amount and purchase or sell products. The equilibrium price at a given moment reflects the crowd's preferences.

Once again, three participants are in play. First there is the organization wishing to conduct the survey. At least three types of stakeholder can participate in this sort of operation: those who are directly concerned by the result; those who traditionally conduct surveys; and current events sites wishing to attract more readers. The second participant, the crowd, is made up, in this case, of anonymous individuals, but it can also be an internal community within an organization. Finally, we have the intermediary – the one who concretely offers the survey, connecting the client and the crowd. These may be independent platforms, but also the publishers of software who provide a development kit the client can integrate into its website. Another particularity of this type of crowdsourcing is that it can be used indirectly; that is, we can observe particular markets that have a link to the principal event, and try to detect how these markets anticipate the result of the principal event. Erikson and Wlezien [WLE 12] clearly show the pertinence of this method of prediction (p. 538):

> "As we show here, early markets worked so well that we are led to believe that the political cognoscenti of the times could read the political tea leaves about as well as modern day observers can from reading the polls."

4.4.2. An illustrative example

A small French startup, Predicti offered a group of surveys on questions related to current events. Let us look at what the site said about itself.[6]

> How does it work?
>
> On Predicti, we want the system to be as simple as possible. It is a predictive market with virtual currency called Predz (the game is completely free to play).
>
> Here, we speculate on the outcome of an event such as an election or a sporting result, through shares of varying value. The value of a share is equal to the probability of occurrence of the event given as a percentage.
>
> Example: Candidate A has a 43% chance of winning the next election. The value of the share "Candidate A wins the election" is then equal to 43 Predz.
>
> You can therefore create plus-values or minus-values by reselling your shares at a value different from the purchase price.

---

6 http://www.predicti.fr/marche-predictif.

When the answer to the question is known, whoever bet on the correct option is paid: all of their winning shares are traded at the maximum price of 100 Predz!

Example: Candidate A is elected, as I predicted by buying 10 shares. These shares are traded to me against 100 Predz per unit, or 1,000 Predz. I bought them at 43 Predz per unit, so in the end I've won 100-430 = 570 Predz.

Why is this of interest?

The predictive market is unarguably the best way to predict the future. Collective intelligence motivated by reward often proves itself to be startlingly accurate, and can rival opinion surveys. This system is based on several assets:

– Transparency: the prediction is directly asked of the participant. There is no need to take a sample.

– The lure of reward: players stake their virtual money are therefore motivated by gain and seek out correct information.

– The "invisible hand" (Adam Smith): in the search for maximum gain, betters react via sale and purchase as soon as there is an interest in it, and tend to form balanced results.

From a practical point of view, the predictive market also has the advantage of reacting in real time and being low-cost compared to surveys.

What can we note from this?

Firstly, we are dealing with fictitious money, which avoids legal hassles and perhaps also biases (though it is still interesting to determine these biases).

Secondly, it is very easy to sign up and participate.

Thirdly, the site is run by young students and is certainly providing them with experience in their studies and for their futures as executives or entrepreneurs.

Though this startup failed after only a few months (largely because the young student who founded it moved on to other projects) the ideas behind it remain relevant and may provide precedents for future entrepreneurs.

4.4.3. *Why it works*

The one we think will win is not necessarily the one we would prefer. In a classic survey, a person indicates his/her preference, and the important thing is to determine a representative sample and one as small as possible for reasons of cost. Here, the goal is to get as many people as possible to participate, without worrying about knowing who they are. The act of choosing the one we think will win will have the effect of taking the undecided fringe into account. Indeed, the die-hard fan of a given candidate will choose this person no matter what, but an undecided person can express his/her doubts by buying and then selling the candidates' "shares".

The game-like aspect of the stock market indisputably attracts gamblers. Gaspoz [GAS 11] has also shown that the act of playing with fictitious money and not "real" money does not influence participation in these markets.

4.4.4. *Limitations*

Occurrences of share-price manipulation as seen in a financial market may limit the use of this method in the public sphere.

In a closed context (a department in an organization, for example), this may lead to the questioning of the power of the head of department, who is normally responsible for making these decisions. How can a manager be useful if he doesn't make the decisions?

4.4.5. *The future*

In one very interesting article, a team of researchers from the University of California have shown how to link data coming from Twitter and the evolution of the share market [RUI 12]. The aim of this study is to show that the link is not from the stock market towards Twitter; on the contrary, from the analysis of Twitter messages towards the market floor. It is, therefore, a form of prediction based on the behavior of a crowd of anonymous individuals. This type of predictive analysis appears highly promising. Indeed, the propensity of the crowd to write about all the events happening in its near or even distant environment is phenomenal. The generation of predictive algorithms might then open up a new field in data analysis, and it is a good bet that specialists in Bayesian analysis will be well-placed to contribute to this [TIC 13; WRI 72]. The sectors impacted could include:

– determination of new consumer needs;

– the cinematographic and gaming industries;

– politics;

– the monitoring of social movements;

– primary materials markets.

In short, this is a method that will be interesting to follow in the coming years.

4.5. Crowdsourcing and innovation

Outsourced activity	Response to mainly technical and sometimes conceptual problems.
Characteristics of outsourced activity	Both the problem and the response must be able to be formalized.
Secondary effects	Some R&D activities may be affected.
Future of this method	This method will continue to develop.
Some examples	Innocentive InnovationExchange

Table 4.6. *Crowdsourcing and innovation summary table*

4.5.1. *What is it?*

A platform may be seen from two angles: as a connecting organization, or as a seller of ideas.

This notion of "idea-selling" might also constitute a new industry for some participants. For example, if a large distributor has a large community of clients, it can use this community as a source of suggestions for new ideas that can then be commercialized.

It can also use the crowd for testing ideas suggested by third-party companies, and then indicate to these third parties whether the ideas are interesting or not. This "idea-seller" function is a service function.

Etymologically speaking, the word "innovation" comes from the Latin (new), which generates the verb *innovare*, defined as:

"[T]he act of introducing into an established situation, something new and unknown."[7]

It is associated with the idea of progress and enjoys a positive and enhancing connotation in Human Sciences. It can be distinguished from "invention" by thinking of it as an economic validation of an invention. Thus, when crowdsourcing participants express expectations in terms of innovation, a value-creator for the organization, this is the dedicated term they use.

To refine this concept that has various, sometimes contradictory meanings, we rely on the following levels of analysis: the nature of the innovation, understood in terms of results or processes; the principal classifications of the innovation; and the reference system used to appreciate novelty [AYE 06; CRO 10; MOR 10].

The nature of the innovation as understood in terms of results or processes

As a result, innovation necessarily presents a "finished" character, whether we are dealing with a technology, a product or a procedure. As a process, innovation is understood in a dynamic manner through

---

7 Merriam Webster dictionary:
http://www.merriam-webster.com/dictionary/innovate?show=0&t=1372241703.

its developments and trajectories. A crowdsourcing operation, then, falls into the category of an organization's innovation process. Its result is constituted of the selection made by either that same organization or by the crowd of one of the latter's productions.

Principal classifications of innovation

There are two classifications; one according to the intrinsic nature of the novelty and one according to the intensity (or degree) of which it is capable.

– Depending on the intrinsic nature of the innovation, a new classification has emerged distinguishing technological innovation from organizational innovation, and product innovation from procedural innovation. Usually assimilated into an internal innovation, organizational innovation particularly concerns formal structures, rules and procedures, and decision-making systems. For this reason, it does not currently involve crowdsourcing operations. Technological innovation concerns both products and procedures, whether they are new or simply improved, and stems more from an external referential (sanction of the market) for the former, and an internal referential (evaluation of the organization) for the latter. Note that crowdsourcing operations deal with both product and procedural innovations.

– The intensity or degree of innovation can be represented on a continuum ranging from radical to incremental. An innovation is qualified as radical when it is based on new knowledge, sometimes completely foreign to traditional know-how. At the other end, an innovation is referred to as incremental when it does not involve fundamentally new knowledge and is based on a progressive improvement of existing knowledge. Expectations with regard to innovative crowdsourcing operation creations are more related to radical innovation; however, as we will see, crowdsourcing can lead to incremental innovations as well.

Reference system used to gauge novelty

Two reference points dominate the literature as end-points on a continuum:

– Organization, or minimal referential, in the context of which innovation occurs when a company does something it has never done before.

– Market, or maximal referential. In this distinction, an innovation is effective only if it is being achieved for the first time in the absolute sense.

The innovative creations expected from crowdsourcing operations are most often judged as such by the organization which is gauging its novelty in reference to itself. When it proposes a challenge, the organization is hoping to benefit from the skills of individuals whose area of expertise is far enough away from its own, in order to obtain innovative solutions thanks to analogical processes or phenomena of transposition. These solutions do not necessarily seem new for the market, but they are new for the organization.

In summary, expectations in terms of innovative creation by a crowdsourcing operation are expressed by the more-or-less radical novelty of a product or procedure, a novelty determined by the organization and obtained via the expertise of individuals in the crowd whose area of expertise is rarely identical to that of the organization.

4.5.2. *Why it works*

As Howe has indicated from the beginning [HOW 06], the crowd is full of specialists. Innovation does not necessarily result from deep reasoning in an area A, but most often from the putting into practice of existing solutions in a remote area called B toward this area A. The key factor for success lies, then, in the ability to create links between people and ideas that are initially quite distant from one another. Here we see the famous concept of the strength of weak links proposed by Granovetter [GRA 73]. Given that it is not naturally possible to predict which domain Y will be the most fruitful in generating innovations in a domain X, only crowdsourcing allows us to find these links. Of course, here again, we cannot be absolutely certain. How then can we increase the chances that an innovation will emerge? We believe a condition and a motivation must be present. The condition is that of the participants' trust in the seriousness and professionalism of the crowdsourcing innovation platform. Let us look again at the notion of trust. Very often, during courses at foreign universities, students or executives attending a seminar on this type of crowdsourcing will say to us: "But he's going to have his idea stolen." This perfectly understandable feeling is deeply anchored in most people's mentalities. However, these students come to understand very quickly the following spiral mechanism: the more the crowdsourcing platform guarantees the fairness and correctness of the transaction, the larger the community of people proposing solutions will become. The larger this population grows, the more interest companies will take in proposing problems to be solved. The more the number of these clients increases, the more revenue the platform will receive. Therefore, it is in the direct interest of the platform to guarantee the security and integrity of transactions. The students then understand that it only takes one "solution-finder" who feels that he/she has been cheated, and who then complains publicly on blogs and other social network media, to scare off the whole community of these "solution-finders" very quickly, thus ruining the platform. For this reason, the legal framework is very precise. As an illustration, the text describing the legal contract is often longer than the text describing the problem to be solved.

With regard to motivation, the client seeking a solution may adjust the amount of the fee they is offering to fit the solution of the problem they are posing. They may even offer a sum greater than the reasonable cost of the solution. In fact, and this is a strong point of this type of outsourcing, when a company has an R&D department, it pays its researchers whether they discover anything or not. There is a fixed cost, then, that must be taken into account. When innovations are crowdsourced, the client pays only if its challenge is resolved; therefore it pays a variable cost and avoids a fixed expense. It can then increase this variable cost in order to boost its chances of receiving a solution, as well as cutting the time it takes for this solution to be obtained.

4.5.3. *Limitations*

Two types of limitation may be cited. Firstly, only problems that can be formalized may then be made available to the crowd. Indeed, the challenge must be written out before it can be diffused. A document must be drafted or a video can be produced. The author must know how to deal subtly with ambiguity. If the text is too specific, it may limit the possibilities for innovation if the person seeking to find a solution ends up feeling as if he/she is trapped in a tunnel. If the text is too ambiguous, and the seekers do not understand what is expected of them well enough, the responses given may be too scattered. Moreover, many problems are difficult to formalize. We recall the example below, taken from the story of a discussion between the director David Lynch and his screenwriter:

> "The writer Barry Gifford, who wrote the book *Wild at Heart*, which was brought to the screen by David Lynch, reports this strange discussion[8]. A few years ago, David Lynch, the producer Monty Montgomery, Vinnie Deserio and I were sitting around a table and talking, when David Lynch tried to explain to me the effect he was after for his next film. He said, 'You know that feeling you have when you've just picked up a pair of Dacron pants from a dye shop? You put your hand in your pocket and you feel something like mashed-up sandwiches all over your fingers. That's the feeling I'm looking for.' I just nodded my head, saying: 'Okay, David, I know exactly what you mean.' And that's how we laid the groundwork for the movie *Lost Highway*."

This example perfectly illustrates the fact that some problems cannot be easily put into words. To conclude, in a recent article in the *Harvard Business Review*, Spradlin [SPR 12] shows clearly that, very often, companies do not spend enough time to adequately define and, especially, formalize their problems.

The second limitation has to do with security. It is always interesting for a company to know its competitors' problems, or more generally, the problems in its field. For a company, revealing its issues may be seen as airing its weaknesses. This feeling is a strong deterrent to using the crowd, and more generally to the Open Innovation phenomenon overall. More underhandedly, a company may display "false" problems to make its competitors believe it has taken a certain route, while in reality it is going in a different direction altogether. Thus, this method of outsourcing can also be fertile ground for the manipulation of information in order to best the competition.

---

8 *Premiere Magazine*, May 2002, p. 114.

4.5.4. *The future*

The future of this method is closely linked to the development of the concept of Open Innovation, and thus to its limitations. We mentioned earlier the question of security and confidentiality. One solution is to create internal innovation platforms. Obviously, this is only of interest to companies of a certain size and which involve varied activities. But let us take the case of a French company such as Sodexo[9]. Its activities are spread out over various sectors, from a French business to the United States Marine Corps. The internal implementation of an Innocentive-type platform could be beneficial for proposing innovations.

With regard to the development of existing solutions, from our perspective the role of trust is essential, and the market should concentrate itself on just a few stakeholders – broadly speaking, Innocentive and several solutions targeting specific issues. It will be interesting to observe whether these types of practices emerge in China and throughout Asia in general.

4.6. Crowdsourcing and authenticity (C&A)

Outsourced activity	The creation of a bond of proximity with its environment.
Characteristics of the outsourced activity	Perceptions concerning either the brand or the company's product. This can also be the perception of an element about which the Internet user feels strongly.
Secondary effects	Classic marketing agents. Press agencies and newspapers.
Future of this method	Solution is small in scope but should endure.
Some examples	Eyeka – France 24 Observateurs. Lionbridge, WHP.

Table 4.7. *Crowdsourcing & authenticity summary table*

9 Number-one leader worldwide in catering and corporate services, with more than 420,000 employees worldwide.

4.6.1. *What is it?*

Every organization has always wanted to understand its environment. In order to do this, a certain proximity is necessary. Traditionally outsourced to companies specializing in opinion surveys, the search for this understanding of the important participants in a company's environment can also be conducted by crowdsourcing.

Thus, C&A consists of outsourcing to a crowd the activity of seeking to understand feelings and tastes concerning an organization, brand or product.

Expectations in terms of authentic creations by crowdsourcing participants are, in the vast majority, connected to a brand (Lego, Dell, Gervais, Kickers, etc.). Therefore, this work is oriented toward brand authenticity.

According to Kolar and Zabkar [KOL 10], brand authenticity can be defined using cognitive or experiential dimensions. The cognitive image shows the beliefs on which consumers seem to rely in establishing the authenticity of a brand. According to this approach, an authentic brand may be defined as a brand perceived as original, anchored in an origin and thus singular, sincere, or possessing authority, as implied by its Greek root-word *authentikos*[10].

If cognitive dimensions appear throughout the literature and business practices to translate brand authenticity, this authenticity also emerges from affective and sensorial elements. From an experiential angle, an authentic brand supposes an intimate or even passionate connection between brand and consumer [GOB 01]. The brand is the catalyst for an experience that transports the consumer into his/her memories [COV 01, p. 78] and/or allows him/her to create or affirm his/her personal identity [MAC 99]. An authentic brand then requires a strong link, a true proximity between the brand and the consumer that will cause the latter to become invested in the brand, to participate in its construction and image-building.

---

10 Merriam Webster dictionary:
http://www.merriam-webster.com/dictionary/authentic.

This effort to define an authentic brand illuminates the expectations of crowdsourcing operators with regard to authentic creations. They want the crowd to give them creations that are unique and original, and therefore authentic in the cognitive sense of the concept. Moreover, they expect the crowd to participate, through its creations, in the construction of the brand's image and identity, which will be all the more authentic the closer the crowd is to the brand. This necessary proximity leads in this case to a reduction of the crowd to brand consumers, with the consequence of transforming the crowd into a clan-community.

In order to develop and nurture the relationship between brand and consumer, experiential marketing approaches make extensive use of the concept of immersion [FOU 98]. Schematically, this is a matter of creating experiential contexts encouraging the immersion of the consumer, such as brand stores, factories, parties, and websites [CAR 06]. Crowdsourcing operations seem to fall well within these experiential contexts created by organizations in order to develop the consumer-brand relationship. In addition, crowdsourcing fulfills a double, self-reinforcing function:

– strengthening of the bond between brand and consumer;

– production and/or selection by the consumer of authentic creations.

The search for proximity can also take the form of translation. Translating a term using only a dictionary precludes taking into account context and sense. To translate well, we must understand and empathize with the way of thinking of the person who wrote the original text. This is why companies such as Lionbridge and WHP use crowdsourcing to improve the quality of massive translations. Of course, the benefits of this are cumulative; that is, not only is there proximity, but the translation operation is carried out more quickly and at less cost.

4.6.2. *Why it works*

There is a belief that new technologies contribute to the cutting of social ties. Remember that when books were first mass-distributed to family homes, many believed that books would destroy all communication within the family circle and transform families into separate individuals, each with heads buried in their own books. The same thinking was applied to the Internet. However, there are several points to note:

– The number of people with whom we can be in relationships, given our cognitive capacities, remains fairly constant. This is the famous Dunbar number [BEN 13].

– The figure of six handshakes[11] established by the Hungarian Frigyes Karinthy tends to drop to four or five with the use of recent social networks.

– Attachment to a brand or to values always remains significant.

Thus, technology will not only *not* destroy bonds, it will offer solutions for creating them, and in addition, an individual will always wish to bond with a brand with which he or she identifies. The profound resiliency of this attachment continues to be studied, particularly in the field of Marketing, and can vary. Here, however, we have both the desire and the means. Thus this method of outsourcing can only succeed – provided, of course, that it is implemented correctly.

4.6.3. *Limitations*

The first limitation is related to the notion of reversal of control.

The theme of control constitutes a vast field of study in Management Science; moreover, it is desirable to have choices concerning the approach we wish to retain. In this examination we will consider the concept of control from the angle of system processing. Cybernetics is a field of research founded largely by Wiener, McCulloch, and Ashby. It can be considered as a science aimed at understanding how systems regulate and control themselves [MIN 10]. More precisely, cybernetics studies the flows of information through a system and the way in which this information is

---

11 "Six Degrees of Separation Theory".

used by the system as a way of controlling itself. In this context, Ashby [ASH 56] proposed his famous law on required variety. By "variety" we mean the counting of the quantity of behaviors and different states proposed by a system. The principle of required variety states that the piloting of a system requires that the directing system be able to implement a wider variety of behaviors than the directed system [BOU 08]. A reversal of control occurs when the variety of the subordinate system increases and exceeds that of the superior system.

The second limitation is related to the intrinsic versatility of the crowd. A client often tends to change his/her tastes in the same way he/she uses a remote control. If a company places the client, or more precisely, his/her perceptions, at the center of its strategy, there is a high risk that it will not be able to follow all the client's changes of mind. The company may then find itself constantly lagging behind, and finally being considered as eternally out-of-date.

4.6.4. The future

Wishing to create secure bonds of proximity with its clients is one of the essential missions of any company. Seeking to understand the feelings of its clients in order to better adapt its offer is also crucial. However, the truth can sometimes be hard to hear, and even harder to integrate. Moreover, tightening bonds and failing to take into account expressed opinions are mutually antagonistic actions. Organizations wishing to benefit from this method of outsourcing must:

– possess the technological skill to create a crowdsourcing bond;

– be in a field likely to encourage this creation of bonds of proximity;

– be flexible enough to adapt when the community's sentiments evolve and strong and convincing enough to explain to this community that it has not understood the message correctly, and that it is therefore going in the wrong direction.

In short, the search for authenticity via crowdsourcing can only involve skilled and agile organizations, and for this reason the development of this method of outsourcing will be limited. The risk of loss of control, as described above, will also limit many companies' use of this manner of creating bonds. On the other hand, quantitative functioning measurements of a community attached to a brand may constitute a new way of measuring the power of that brand. For example, if a brand of Brittany cakes has a community of 10,000 Internet users in certain cities throughout the world who participate regularly in marketing operations, this means that the brand is more valued than its net profit alone may lead us to think. In this sense, the development of crowdsourcing as part of a quest for authenticity can be considered as a way of showing the value of a brand to potential investors. We believe this type of use to be highly promising.

4.7. Crowdauditing

Outsourced activity	Data analysis aimed at finding problems or opportunities.
Characteristics of outsourced activity	Data must be in a usable format. Data can spread across several domains in order to show correlations.
Secondary effects	Business activities based on private data sources may be affected.
Future of this method	The challenges are political, but this type of method promises strong development.
Some examples	Data.gouv.fr France Open Data Paris Data Publica Extractive Industries Transparency Initiative Enel

Table 4.8. *Crowdauditing summary table*

4.7.1. *What is it?*

This method of crowdsourcing is closely correlated to the development of the Open Data movement we discussed at the beginning of this book.

The general idea of crowdauditing lies in the outsourcing by an organization of the analysis of its business data. What types of organizations may be involved? Of course, the first thought is of large organizations, particularly public organizations. In this case, the auditing of data is aimed primarily at detecting any anomalies in the organization's functioning. Secondly, this type of audit may bring to light business opportunities for the crowdauditors. For example, the analysis of train and bus schedules near a station can reveal unavoidable waiting times for travelers making connections, but also periods of flow. Thus, it becomes possible for a taxi company to pre-position its taxis during the most profitable times and avoid lost time for its drivers, and to limit the number of people unable to find a taxi.

However, private organizations can also use this method. In the context of transparency policies and in order to show an organization's desire to allow its clients to participate in its workings, business data may be made available.

The welcome page of the American website MCC (Millennium Challenges Corporation[12]) provides a good description of this type of outsourcing.

These data are provided as part of MCC's commitment to transparency and accountability, to improve access to development and aid data and expand the creative use of that data beyond the walls of government. We hope to spark your imagination and spur the creation of innovative web applications, data visualizations and analyses.

---

12 http://data.mcc.gov/.

An example from Goldcorp:

The Canadian gold mining group Goldcorp made 400 megabytes of geological survey data on its Red Lake, Ontario, property available to the public over the Internet. They offered a $575,000 prize to anyone who could analyze the data and suggest places where gold could be found. The company claims that the contest produced 110 targets, over 80% of which proved productive; yielding 8 million ounces of gold, worth more than $3 billion. The prize was won by a small consultancy in Perth, Western Australia, called Fractal Graphics.

4.7.2. Why it works

It is always tempting to rummage through someone else's data. The "investigative" instinct possessed by many people is a powerful driving force. It seems to work especially well in exposing an organization's weaknesses. The number of Internet sleuths searching for faults is particularly high. Simply compare this mechanism with the model that prevails in computer security. The world of hackers is vast, with all of them seeking to understand a system and cause it to malfunction. In the context of an audit of open data, the same behavior can be put to work.

One recent initiative is worthy of mention: the case of the company Crowdstrike. This computer security company relies on a "community to help a community", as stated in its introductory video by George Kurtz, the CEO. A community of individuals points out security flaws so that the community of users can prepare for and resist attacks. Computer security is a problem that is often presented as being very technical and reserved for a few shadowy figures in the know. However, the democratization of analysis tools and the desire to overcome a challenge has led to a large number of people being able to participate in this security (on the sides of both attackers and defenders).

In his introductory speech, George Kurtz says:

> "I don't think this is just the technology issue, that can solve this problem, I think that it is a human issue and people need to help each other."[13]

The original idea is based on the realization that a community of hackers cannot be defeated with technological solutions alone; rather, the deeper motivations of the hackers must be used to develop a community that will be evenly matched against this "bad" community. This will involve the inspection of millions of pieces of connection data to find attacks in progress: this is crowdauditing.

The second cause of crowdauditing's success lies in the search for financial opportunity. Indeed, a large part of many organizations' data is an unutilized resource. Imagine a hotel with a breakfast room that is somewhat cramped and cannot be enlarged because renovations are expensive. Depending on the percentage of clients who eat their breakfast in the hotel or not, and depending on the hotel's rate of frequentation, it might be of interest for a nearby bakery to produce more or fewer croissants in the morning. Agreements between these two businesses (the hotel and the bakery) may be imagined. The hotel's interest would be in finding a partner to offer a complete service to its clients, and the bakery would increase its own clientele.

4.7.3. Limitations

The main limitation of crowdauditing is that the number of organizations deciding to open up their data is drying up. It is a bit like going to the doctor; when he begins to look for potential problems he will generally find several, even though the patient feels perfectly healthy. Certain illnesses may very well never appear, but now the patient knows he is at risk, and his future life will be affected by this. Likewise, some companies have no desire for their weaknesses to be exposed, as this will certainly change the way their investors view them.

---

13 http://www.crowdstrike.com/index.html.

Here too, we might mention a more insidious limitation, one related to the handling of transmitted data. To make a person trust in a solution, the best strategy is to let him or her find it for him/herself. This does not mean releasing false data, but rather being very careful about the way in which data is made available. The crowd must be allowed to find by itself correlations that shed a positive light on a field or an organization. Of course, this type of strategy is extremely risky, since if it is revealed, it will cause long-term damage to the image of the organization providing the data. However, it should not be ruled out.

4.7.4. *The future*

The future of this method is partly dependent on the development of Open Data. We are somewhat pessimistic about the current public Open Data boom. Simply look at the figures: in the year 2011 alone, 350,000 datasets were released. By April 2013, there were only 353,226 datasets available. It seems that the openness movement has slowed down to a large extent. The causes of this are difficult to pinpoint, but one of them may lie in the fact that in order to distribute "clean" data in an open format, a company must possess this type of data to begin with, and if it does not, there are perhaps implications as to the limitations of the internal data architecture of some administrations.

With regard to the future of the liberalization of private data for audit by the crowd, we are again fairly pessimistic. In fact, we are reminded of the OpenBook Management movement, which took place 20 years ago. In this case, accounting data was made available to all employees so that they could manage financial matters more easily and better understand their company as a whole [CAS 96; CAS 98]. However, the reality is that this did not end up being a phenomenon shared by all; the data remained highly confidential. This example does not give us great confidence in the future of the crowdauditing of private data.

4.8. Crowdcontrol

Outsourced activity	The security of people and goods.
Characteristics of outsourced activity	The concept of real time is important since it is a question of detecting and reacting quickly to a breach of security.
Secondary effects	Traditional surveillance companies.
Future of this method	It is being led to develop and become more widespread with the increased lack of security.
Some examples	Kaspersky Anti-cybercriminalité

Table 4.9. *Crowdauditing summary table*

4.8.1. *What is it?*

"Today, the Manchester police force can no longer avoid social networking; it has become part of daily life. The Manchester police department has 60 Twitter accounts and 50 Facebook accounts, and each local station has one of its own."

These were the words of Kevin Hoy, officer and webmaster for the Manchester police department in the United Kingdom, at a conference entitled "Information and Communication Technologies and Public Order" during the 5th International Forum on Cybersecurity in Lille on Tuesday, January 28, 2013. What is the purpose of this social networking presence? The answer is simple: to collect information and pass messages on to the crowd. Indeed, within this crowd there are both potential victims and possible informers. China, with its website 12309, is even offering a unique platform allowing individuals who have been victims of corruption to point the finger at unscrupulous civil servants. The English website Internet Eyes[14] also uses this principle, with the addition of a well-thought-out interface

---

14 http://www.interneteyes.co.uk/.

and a somewhat surprising business model. Here, Internet users are invited to pay a fee in order to watch CCTV footage (£1.99 per month, or £15.99 per year), and if they witness a crime or misdemeanor they may warn the appropriate authorities. They will then receive a fee (£10) when they detect abnormal behavior. This results in a profit once two crimes or misdemeanors have been reported.

Thus, crowdsecurity can be defined as the outsourcing to a crowd of surveillance and security activities.

One French startup even tried two years ago to propose a system composed as follows: on one end, people feeling unsafe were given a small case containing a GSM chip and an alarm button. On the other end were private security officers with mobile telephones. These agents were not bound by any specific commitment and could turn off this telephone whenever they wished, particularly when they were occupied in other, traditional security work. The functioning principle was that when a client felt threatened, he/she pressed the button, and the nearest officer(s) received a text with the nominative information and precise location of the person needing aid. They would then travel to the site and dissuade the threatening individual by their presence. This idea did not come to fruition for reasons of practicality, but it remains interesting as an example of crowdcontrol.

4.8.2. *Why it works*

This type of crowdsourcing can only succeed for the following reasons:

– civic-mindedness;

– curiosity, sometimes to the point of voyeurism;

– a small reward but one that can be highly valued (the role of rescuer).

4.8.3. *Limitations*

There are several limitations worthy of note. Firstly, and particularly in France, security and control are tasks that are part of public services. The idea of leaving these tasks to individuals, especially individuals who are anonymous, is likely to meet strong resistance.

Secondly, there is a whole legal framework that must be put in place, as a member of the crowd can never be duly sworn, and it seems problematic to base any type of justice-related action on such a mechanism.

Thirdly, crowdcontrol could be considered harmful to public order by creating a permanent state of suspicion. It does not take much to turn a community into a vigilante group, and this is a highly dangerous eventuality.

Fourthly, this method could, of course, be used in order to guarantee the security of our fellow citizens, but it could easily be manipulated in order to get around the law. Radar-detection systems are an example of this. Indeed, the exchanging of radar-beacon locations by members of a community of drivers allows some people to slow down when necessary and speed up (at their own risk) when they can. This mechanism is clearly a type of crowdcontrol, but its positioning with regard to respecting the rules of the road may be subject to debate. The iPhone application called "ticket", which allows the sharing of information about the position of subway ticket-checkers in certain French cities, stems from the same logic.

4.8.4. *The future*

Despite its numerous limitations, we believe this method to have a bright future, and one that should be developed quite rapidly, and in part by public authorities, even though the reporting of information must be done very carefully. Crowdcontrol is a powerful tool able to assist with the burden of public order. The recent case of the role of Reddit in the tracking of the two Boston terrorists in April 2013 is an illustrative example of this. Using the power of the crowd may balance out the asymmetry of some security crises [COU 02]. With regard to private organizations, new methods remain to be invented, with one objective being to ensure security in stores, for example by reducing theft. The analysis of flows of information stemming from social networks (especially Twitter) could be used to deal with social movements endangering an organization's activity [DEN 13].

At the community level, we believe that the fact that everyone possesses at least one connected device will lead to flourishing developments in crowdcontrol. The best ideas (meant to ensure a peaceful life) as well as the worst (to evade the law) are yet to come. From our perspective, this specific point will be a major question for society in the years to come.

4.9. Crowdcuration

Outsourced activity	Classification of data, information, and knowledge.
Characteristics of outsourced activity	Requires the general theme to be attractive.
Secondary effects	Employees responsible for this task; certain companies selling publicity materials or surveys on a theme; journalists.
Future of this method	Will likely grow and be of interest to various types of companies.
Some examples	The film "Life in day" on Youtube Wikipedia

Table 4.10. *Crowdcuration summary table*

4.9.1. *What is it?*

The term "curation" means the organization of content in order subsequently to reveal relevant information. Diversity of content makes this a highly arduous task.

If an organization wishes to undertake this project internally, it must designate a person or a team to carry out the tasks presented by Bhargava [BHA 10] as follows:

– define an area of interest;

– select the sources to be examined;

– verify the reliability of content;

– cite the authors;

– create a network with experts in the field;

– write editorials;

– ergonomically present the content gathered;

– share the structured content on various networks;

– analyze reader profiles.

Thus, crowdcuration means, for an organization, outsourcing the activity of generating, grouping, and sorting data pertaining to specific subjects. It is thus a task of arranging, which can be justified by the endlessly growing volumes of data.

4.9.2. *An illustrative example*

As Chris Riback wrote on his blog in 2012:

> "With just 10 days to go until our nation comes together to choose our next President, we already have a winner in this election: social media and crowdsourced news. The days of waiting for a bunch of editors or TV talking heads to tell us what is important are gone. Today, information trends – and the news that gets the most likes, posts, plus 1's...in other words, the more information goes viral, that's what the headlines will be. And it's driven much of the political coverage, just as it will once the election is through. And the leader in this trending form of trending information is BuzzFeed."[15]

The information website BuzzFeed stands, we believe, as an example of the perfect combined use of crowd, experts and technologies.

---

15 http://chrisriback.com/tag/crowdsourcing/.

The crowd of poster: sends photos, videos, text captures, and various other elements, the interest of which (or lack thereof) can be quickly measured.

Experts (editors and journalists) will then cite some of the above media (or not). They will also write articles related to the items of this media in which the crowd of readers has shown the most interest.

The crowd of readers will then react to the documents posted by sharing or ignoring them.

Information technologies: BuzzFeed has created algorithms analyzing the behavior of the crowd of readers and assigning icons categorizing the documents shared. The range of feedback options is wider than a simple "I like this" or "I don't like this", as shown in the figure below:

Figure 4.5. *Buzzfeed categories*

The result is a snapshot of current events that, to date, has had more than 30 million unique users each month, with a staff of only about a hundred people. In the field of advertising the site is also an innovator, using participation analysis to increase its number of clicks.

4.9.3. *Why it works*

The human capacity for recognition remains greater in many cases to that of machines. A good example is that of Microsoft's research projects to develop traditional text recognition in "Captcha". The ASIRRA project[16] proposes to verify whether one is dealing with a man or a machine by showing a dozen images of either dogs or cats. The person being tested must click, for example, on the cat photos. This task, which is easy for a human, is much harder for a machine. In

---

16 http://research.microsoft.com/en-us/um/redmond/projects/asirra/.

addition, if a system is well thought-out; that is, if it motivates the user sufficiently to associate categories with the elements proposed, this system will be effective.

The second reason for this method's success lies in a certain human inclination to arrange, classify, and box up the things around us. This phenomenon has been studied in psychology, neurology, and even the field of art [GOM 02]. Even in the domain of decision-making, the naturalist approach is based on the decision-maker's first impression of a situation. Faced with a problematic situation, the expert decision-maker will immediately associate what he sees with an analogous situation he has already encountered [KLE 98]. This capacity for categorization is innate. Thus, in a crowd, there will be people who tirelessly arrange, sort and categorize the jumble in front of them. Note that this desire to arrange can be effective even if the site is not considered ergonomic. The venerable example of the Craigslist bulletin-board website is a good example of this. There are pre-existing categories, but people can point out whether this or that posting is in the right category, and thus it is possible to have a quality-control service even with a site that is visually very simple.

In short, crowdcuration works because humans have the innate ability and motivation to put things away.

4.9.4. *Limitations*

The principal limitation of this method is that it only involves subjects for which there is sufficient traffic. Indeed, out of the volume of people visiting a website, only a small percentage of these individuals will tidy up and thus contribute to the quality of the site. If this volume is too low, there will not be enough "curators" and thus the "mess" will scare away other Internet users, reducing traffic still further. Thus, crowdcuration is applicable to subjects of general interest and limits very specialized initiatives. If a company wishes very specific data to be sorted, it cannot use this method. For example, a university desiring to have its educational content sorted by the crowd will not have an easy task.

4.9.5. *The future*

The future of crowdauditing seems certain, but it also seems restricted to specific areas. What new directions, then, can this method of outsourcing take? More precisely, what themes and communities may be interested in curation?

The fact that crowdauditing requires themes that are interesting to people provides us with part of our answer. Indeed, if the theme is interesting there will be a high output of content and subsequently a great need for sorting. We believe a positive spiral exists here, as shown in the figure below:

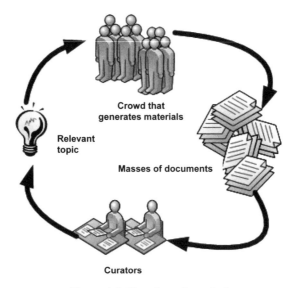

Figure 4.6. *Crowdcuration spiral*

Obviously, certain sectors will take an interest in this method, particularly the news media, but we must also imagine that sectors such as the socio-economic analysis of a country by strategic intelligence organizations may also take advantage of this opportunity. In this context, we believe that crowdcuration is a means of managing what has been referred to as info-obesity [BRO 12]. This neologism harks back to the fact that organizations are not only drowning in data, information and knowledge, they are asking for more. This means that there are more ways of collecting information in existence than there are ways of processing it. Much like overweight individuals, these organizations are less mobile. The only feasible way to manage this info-obesity, we believe, is to call on the crowd, and this is the way to the future.

4.10. Crowdcare

Outsourced activity	The health and protection of individuals.
Characteristics of outsourced activity	Necessity for compassion.
Secondary effects	Personal service companies.
Future of this method	It is likely to develop and become more widespread with the aging of the population and the high cost of managing this issue.
Some examples	*Arrêt Cardiaque* (Heart Attack)

Table 4.11. *Crowdcare summary table*

4.10.1. *What is it?*

The concept of "care" is relatively familiar and simple to understand, but it is often bandied about as it is tied up with political concerns [GIL 08]. Care is fundamentally a reflection on the role of care for others; a well-meaning empathy combined with concrete assistance. In this context, the crowd, aided by technology, can bring aid to people in difficulty. The members of a crowd may, for example, comfort individuals in distress via material assistance or simply via messages. The outsourced activities are those handled by government services or associations that provide constant assistance to certain categories of the population. This help may be health-related, emotional, material, etc.

4.10.2. *An illustrative example*

Let us use the example of cardiac arrest in France. It has been demonstrated that in order to save a person having a heart attack, the use of a defibrillator as soon as possible is necessary. More than 30,000 people die in France each year; only 3 to 4% of heart-attack victims are saved. An association founded by the owners of the media organization RMC/BFM[17] has launched a project that may to a certain extent be considered crowdcare. It was originally an effort to make defibrillators freely available in public places. Next, a smartphone application was developed. This application, called "Heart Attack", has already been downloaded 350,000 times. It allows anyone to act in case of cardiac arrest and to geo-locate the nearest defibrillator. To date, the application has accumulated an inventory of more than 21,000 defibrillators. This is a community tool, and it is the users who contribute to the database by communicating the installation of new defibrillators. In fact, this installation is often dependent on municipal initiatives or the efforts of local associations, and it is therefore quite difficult to get a precise count of the devices being installed. The people who use this application are called "Good Samaritans". The Good Samaritan is a person who is located geographically close to a heart-attack victim and who can intervene rapidly at the site of the incident in order to help the victim's chances of survival while waiting for the arrival of emergency medical care.

Speed of intervention is a crucial component. It is believed that there are only 4 minutes within which to act in case of cardiac arrest. After this period, every additional minute reduces the chances of survival by 10%.

The schema below illustrates this mechanism and shows the role of crowdcare.

---

17 http://www.associationrmcbfm.fr/.

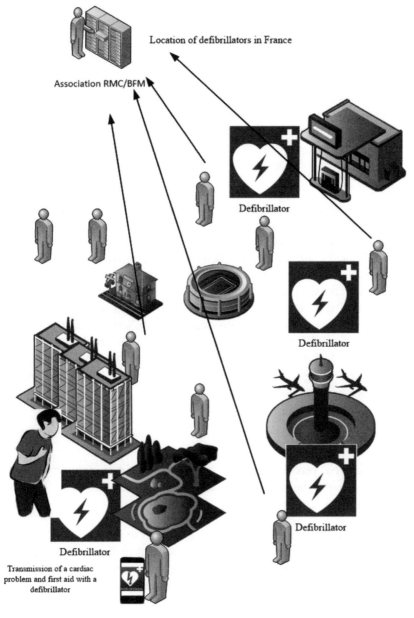

Location of defibrillators in France

Association RMC/BFM

Defibrillator

Defibrillator

Defibrillator

Defibrillator

Transmission of a cardiac
problem and first aid with a
defibrillator

Good Samaritan

Figure 4.7. *Medical crowdcare operation*

4.10.3. *Why it works*

Obviously, the idea of personal compassion for others is a powerful driving force behind this method. In an individualist society, we may also say that this is a low price to pay for a person's life, as well as a method that can benefit a whole community. Finally, we can each say to ourselves: "I'd like someone to do that for me if I were in a crisis." Helping others, then, is a bit like helping ourselves.

4.10.4. *Limitations*

Here again, we find the passionate/skilled dichotomy. Indeed, giving medical assistance requires skill; in some cases care, given incorrectly, can prove dangerous. This care can be medical or psychological; and of course, activities that require advanced skill cannot be outsourced. The risk is that a person will provide help which will prove inadequate and cause complications, and that the person who was assisted might bring a complaint against his or her Samaritan. Note as well that, on this operation's website, it is clearly stipulated that: "You risk only saving a life by responding positively (article 122-7 of the criminal code)."[18] The effect would be disastrous, and the resulting loss of confidence might lead to all crowdcare operations being called into question.

4.10.5. *The future*

It may be possible to pair participation in certain crowdcare operations with the earning of certificates or tests, such as first-aid certificates, for example.

In addition, this method could be extended to include all social aid activities and could be directed at the national or European level, for example. We might imagine a French citizen having a problem in Italy and turning to this method, and another French citizen living in Italy coming to his or her assistance.

---

18 http://www.arretcardiaque.org/devenez-bon-samaritain/.

5

The Dangers of Crowdsourcing

Though we are optimistic, every innovation can have a dark side. The aim of this chapter is to imagine and explore the ways in which this dark side might be manifested in the case of crowdsourcing.

Like every managerial method, crowdsourcing may be used for malicious purposes, or diverted toward unaccountable shores.

The first important danger, we believe, is ethical. Crowdsourcing may be seen as a way of "draining the population of its ideas" to benefit a single participant, and thus of impoverishing a whole ecosystem, as suggested by our reading of an excellent interview of Tim O'Reilly in *Wired* magazine.[1] In this interview, the behavior of some Internet users is compared to that of unscrupulous fishermen who practice overfishing and end up stripping an entire ecosystem for short-term profit. This phenomenon is harmful for the environment, but also for the very staying power of these organizations. Similarly, by leading organizations to deal with immense crowds without precautions or safeguards, crowdsourcing can damage the environment within which it is practiced.

---

1 http://www.wired.com/business/2012/12/mf-tim-oreilly-qa/all/.

The second danger is related to "the foolishness of crowds". We have spoken of the wisdom of crowds, but opportunities to observe stupid acts led by crowds are frequent as well.

Let us give a relatively old example in illustration of this statement. In March 2009, a company wished to organize a "buzz" in order to gain recognition for itself. It announced that, on one Saturday afternoon, it would distribute in the streets of Paris 5,000 small red packets containing publicity flyers and cash, ranging from €5 to €500. A huge amount of media attention was paid to this operation, intended to promote Mailorama.fr (a French "cash-back" website). Large groups of people gathered at the planned distribution points, particularly one near the Eiffel Tower. Faced with the volume of the crowd and fearing misbehavior, the decision was made to cancel the operation. This was the starting point for violence and public disruption. The French government subsequently wished to bring legal action against the company to force it to pay for damages. Finally, a few months later, the head of the parent company (called Rentabiliweb) apologized on the radio and offered a sum of money to a charitable organization.

This example emphasizes the dangers of turning to the crowd, and calls into question whether crowdsourcing might bring out the darker side of the crowd: personal greed.

Thirdly, crowdsourcing has so far been presented from the angle of the outsourcing of legal activities by organizations that are also legal. However, criminal organizations have also taken advantage of this opportunity. When this happens, the advantages of crowdsourcing can also be construed as many difficulties that police must overcome. For example, the size of the crowd can be used to reduce the margin of a product while conserving the same result due to an increased volume of sales. It becomes a matter of interest for a network to stop selling drugs and to sell illegal medication instead, as it is far less risky and very profitable to build a vast network for the reselling of medication at low cost. The distribution of resellers all over the world allows certain difficulties with business regulations to be avoided. In addition, in the event of arrest, the penalty for reselling medication is less severe than that for drug dealing.

Fourthly, in 2006, Howe proposed five characteristics to describe the crowd [HOW 06]. We believe one more should be added now: the crowd belongs to networks. It is not composed of millions of tiny, separate grains of sand, but rather of multitudes of stars and planets belonging to systems and galaxies. In reality, most individuals belong to at least one massive social network, and are linked to other people within these networks. This mechanism has a significant impact similar to what financiers call cascades of information [WEL 00]. For Bikhchandani, Hirshleifer, and Welch [BIK 92], a cascade of information means that individuals assign more weight to outside information coming from other members of the crowd than to internal information – that is, information generated by their own reflections. Therefore, in the context of the selection of content by a crowdsourcing operation, a person will not vote "yes" because he or she likes the content to which he/she has been exposed, but rather because one or more people around him/her has voted "yes". This is how opinion-makers appear within groups or networks; their role can prove very harmful and deeply disruptive to the smooth workings of crowdsourcing. Trying to protect a community from "information cascade" mechanisms seems very difficult. It is important to keep in mind that a company cannot control all the information flowing between members of its community. Thus a company can only try to analyze data from the community in order to find some patterns that may show that a cascade is occurring. From our point of view, this is a highly relevant field for future research.

6

The Future of Crowdsourcing

As we have described it in this book, crowdsourcing concerns any activity that is able to be broken down and that can benefit from the diversity of a large number of people. On the other hand, the expansion of the virtual world towards the real world is still in process. Undoubtedly, an innovation proposed on Innocentive will subsequently take material form. For example, a new product may be launched based on the proposed innovation. However, there is a discontinuity in this process, as shown in Figure 6.1.

Crowdsourcing results in the suggestion of ideas that must then be transformed into products. This transformation phase has traditionally been managed by manufacturing facilities. The distribution circuit of the manufactured products to the crowd of clients is classic as well. Take the example of the manufacturing of logos for t-shirts. The design portion of production will be carried out as part of a crowdsourcing operation (as on Threadless, for example). However, the manufacture and distribution of the t-shirts will remain traditional.

As Chris Anderson has brilliantly explained [AND 12], the democratization of two new technologies – 3D printers and laser-cutting machines – has changed the game.

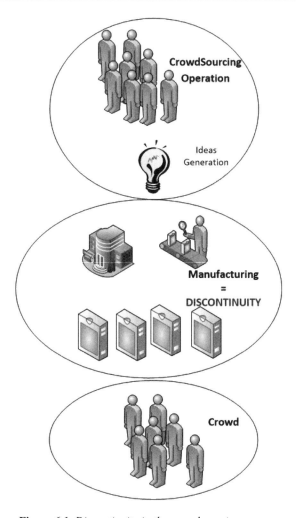

Figure 6.1. *Discontinuity in the crowdsourcing process*

These types of device, connected to PCs with CAD (Computer Aided Design) software and then connected to the Internet, cause the above-mentioned discontinuity to disappear. As with all new phenomena, it is difficult to measure the scope of this method, but its users already have a name: "Makers" (p. 21). Anderson lists the three characteristics of Makers as follows:

1. People using digital desktop tools to create designs for new products and prototype them ("digital DIY").

2. A cultural norm to share those designs and collaborate with others in online communities.

3. The use of common design file standards that allow anyone, if they desire, to send their designs to commercial manufacturing services to be produced in any number, just as easily as they can fabricate them on their desktop. This radically foreshortens the path from idea to entrepreneurship, just as the Web did in software, information, and content.

It is fascinating to observe that Anderson's descriptions fall perfectly within the course of the crowdsourcing movement. Indeed, crowdsourcing is a democratization of the creation of ideas, and Makers are a democratization of the creation of products. These two movements cannot but line up with one another; they share the same spirit, and above all the same effectiveness.

The figure below shows the expansion of the crowdsourcing domain made possible by the democratization of production tools.

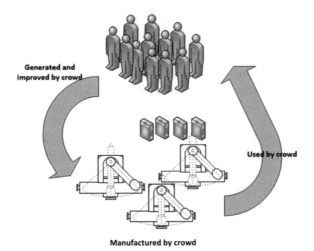

Figure 6.2. *Expansion of the crowdsourcing domain: from the mind via bits down to the atom*

Here are two general examples:

The first example is an imaginary website; it does not exist, but it is a good illustration of this process. The site, which we will call "myrocknrollring.com", sells fashion jewelry. It displays folders containing all sorts of rings. Certain Internet users group these designs according to their taste by voting for them or marking them. The Internet users can then download the file, available in several compatible formats,[1] and then make their own ring at home. They can also suggest variants of these models and post them on the site. Of course, this business model requires further refinement in order for mryrocknrollring.com to be profitable.

The second example is real, and a bit disturbing. In October 2012, *Wired* magazine stated that Cody Wilson, a 25-year-old law student at the University of Texas, proposed putting a model online that would allow a pistol to be made at home with a 3D printer.[2] In December, the same magazine named this young student as one of its 15 most dangerous people. The first prototype was tested in May 2013, and if this model is widely distributed, there is a great risk of it being improved and that a proliferation of more and more innovative handguns will occur.

Having given these two examples, let us return to the links between crowdsourcing and production. The crowdsourcing of production is a way to avoid red tape. Anderson (p. 57) provides a before-and-after snapshot of personal manufacturing technologies. In the "before" state, three conditions must be fulfilled.

The product must be popular enough to be able to be manufactured. Personal manufacturing technologies allow us to avoid this limitation: a product that interests only a few people can easily be manufactured at a constant cost. If the product becomes popular, a traditional mode of manufacture (based on economies of scale) will become necessary. Conversely, a product that interests a few specialists scattered over the globe is perfectly suited to the personal manufacturing model. It becomes easy to have this product

---

1 OBJ, PLY, STL, SKP, 3DS, ZPR, ASE, IGES, DWG, WRL, DEA, IGES, IGS, STEP, STP, etc.
2 http://www.wired.com/dangerroom/2012/10/3d-gun-blocked/.

manufactured by a 3D facility near the client (if he or she does not possess the necessary machinery). It is also possible to have several variants of the product manufactured in the same place and at the same unit cost.

Secondly, the product must be popular enough to be transported and routed by sellers. This limitation becomes meaningless, however, when the only component being transported is the computer design model. Moreover, this transmission has no particular limitations in itself and its cost is negligible.

Finally, the third criterion is that the product must be popular enough for people to be able to know about its existence. The development and business use of search engines has made information pertaining to products especially easy to find.

After the appearance of personal production technologies, all of the conditions are present to eliminate these three types of obstacles. In this context, crowdsourcing is the device that allows us to bypass these limitations:

– outsourcing of production to a crowd of people possessing 3D printers or laser-cutting machines;

– outsourcing of creativity via the sharing of models within the crowd, and thus universal transmission of these models;

– outsourcing of micro-publicity by the crowd.

As we can see, crowdsourcing is not the cause of this phenomenon of democratization of production, but rather the commercial engine.

This future evolution allows us to complete the figure above (see Figure 3.4) by adding the following chart:

	Crowd	Expert
Content Generation	1	2
Content Selection	3	4
Product Manufacturing	5	6

Table 6.1. *Crowd and expert in a crowdsourcing and manufacturing operation*

These six cases constitute so many possibilities available to an organization, and each route so many opportunities to manage an activity. Take, for example, the route 1-4-5. The crowd proposes ideas for new products; the company selects those that it feels are the most relevant, and makes files containing models available to the crowd. The crowd then manufactures these products.

The following routes may be considered:

– 1-3-6: full-crowdsourcing process;

– 1-4-6 or 2-4-6: half-crowdsourcing process;

– 2-4-5: crowdmanufacturing process alone;

– 1-4-5 or 2-3-5: half-crowdsourcing / half-crowdmanufacturing process;

– 1-3-5: full-crowdsourcing and manufacturing process.

As we can see, we now have access to a wide variety of processes in comparison with the traditional 2-4-6 process.

Conclusion

A final reflection

Now that we have arrived at the end of our journey through the land of crowdsourcing, we would like to reflect on three final points linking an organization to a crowd.

– Is crowdsourcing not really just another way of insourcing?[1] With crowdsourcing, the crowd becomes an integral part of the company – an essential connected resource, virtual to be sure, but fundamentally linked to the company all the same.

– Are we on the path to a change in paradigm, the atomization of work, the calling into question of the idea of an employee as we know it, and a return to task – or mission-based work? Indeed, in these times of crisis, why work for one company when we can work for several at once? And, from the company's point of view, why work with only a small number of people when a whole crowd of employees is available?

– According to Actor-Network theory [CAL 06; LAT 92], all types of actors in a network must be taken into account. Humans, machines and documents all create a network that exists, evolves, increases in strength and, sometimes, disappears. Most connected devices are able to be programmed so that they work together; the concept of the crowd requires the enrichment as the above-mentioned concept of the

---

1 http://www.wired.com/wiredenterprise/2013/01/st_essay-insourcing/.

actor. This new form of crowdsourcing / crowdmanufacturing will be a prolific source of opportunity in years to come. Future debates, both managerial and academic, should be rich indeed.

Bibliography

[AGU 07] AGUILA-OBRA A.R.D., PADILLA-MELÉNDEZ A., SERAROLS-TARRÉS C., "Value creation and new intermediaries on Internet. An exploratory analysis of the online news industry and the web content aggregators", *International Journal of Information Management*, 27(3), p. 187-199, 2007.

[AMI 01] AMIT R., ZOTT C., "Value Creation in e-Business", *Strategic Management Journal*, 22, p. 493-520, 2001.

[AND 06] ANDERSON C., *The Long Tail: Why the Future of Business Is Selling Less of More*, New York: Hyperion, 2006.

[AND 12] ANDERSON C., *Makers: The New Industrial Revolution*, New York: Random House - Crown Publishing Group, 2012.

[ARN 00] ARNOLD U., "New dimensions of outsourcing: a combination of transaction cost economics and the core competencies concept", *European Journal of Purchasing & Supply Management*, 6(1), p. 23-29, 2000.

[ASH 56] ASHBY, W. R., *An Introduction to Cybernetics*, New York: John Wiley and Sons, 1956.

[AYE 06] AYERBE C., "Innovation technologique et organisationnelle au sein de P.M.E. innovantes: complémentarité des processus, analyse comparative des mécanismes de diffusion", *Revue Internationale PME*, 19(1), p. 9-34, 2006.

[BAN 09] BANERJI A., DUTTA B., "Local network externalities and market segmentation", *International Journal of Industrial Organization*, 27(5), p. 605-614, 2009.

[BAR 91] BARNEY J., "Firm resources and sustained competitive advantage", *The Journal of Management*, 17(1), p. 99-120, 1991.

[BAR 12] BARTON D., COURT D., "Making Advanced Analytics Work For You", *Harvard Business Review*, 90(10), p. 78-83, 2012.

[BEL 09] BELL D., *The Crowdsourcing Handbook: The How to on Crowdsourcing, Complete Expert's Hints and Tips Guide by the Leading Experts, Everything You Need to Know About Crowdsourcing*, Emereo Pty Limited, 2009.

[BEN 13] BENNETT D., "The Dunbar Number", *Bloomberg Businessweek*, (4312), p. 52-56, 2013.

[BHA 10] BHARGAVA R., "Content Curation: Why Is The Content Curator The Key Emerging Online Editorial Role Of The Future?", http://www.masternewmedia.org/content-curation-why-is-the-content-curator-the-key-emerging-online-editorial-role-of-the-future/, 2010.

[BIK 92] BIKHCHANDANI S., HIRSHLEIFER D., WELCH I., "A Theory of Fads, Fashion, Custom, and Cultural Change as Informational Cascades", *The Journal of Political Economy*, 100(5), 1992.

[BLU 11] BLUENOVE, Open Data: quels enjeux et opportunités pour l'entreprise?, 2011.

[BOU 13] BOUDREAU K. J., LAKHANI K. R., "Using the Crowd as an Innovation Partner", *Harvard Business Review*, 91(4), p. 60-69, 2013.

[BOU 08] BOURION C.,"Les représentations créatives dans la maitrîse de la destinée humaine. Comment les représentations créatives, en accroissant la variété requise de ses comportements, permettent-elles à l'homme augmenté d'accomplir son destin post-moderne?", *Revue Internationale de Psychosociologie*, XIV(1), p. 45-66, 2008.

[BOU 12] BOUTY I., GODÉ C., DRUCKER-GODARD C., NIZET J., PICHAULT F., LIÈVRE P., "Coordination Practices in Extreme Situations", *European Management Journal*, 30(6), p.475-489, 2012.

[BRO 12] BROWN S., "Coping with information obesity: A diet for information professionals", *Business Information Review*, 29(3), p. 168-173, 2012.

[CAL 06] CALLON M., FERRARY M., "Les réseaux sociaux à l'aune de la théorie de l'acteur-réseau", *Sociologies Pratiques*, 2(6), 37-44, 2006.

[CAR 08] CARDON D., "Le design de la visibilité: Un essai de cartographie du web 2.0", *Réseaux* (152), p. 93-137, 2008.

[CAR 06] CARU A., COVA B., "Expériences de marque: comment favoriser l'immersion du consommateur?", *Décision Marketing*, 41, p. 43-52, 2006.

[CAS 96] CASE J. F., *Open-Book Management: The Coming Business Revolution*, Harper Business, 1996.

[CAS 99] CASE J. F., *The Open-Book Experience: Lessons from over 100 Companies Who Successfully Transformed Themselves*, Ann Arbour, USA: Perseus Books, 1999.

[CHA 12] CHANDRA Y., LEENDERS M.A.A.M., "User innovation and entrepreneurship in the virtual world: A study of Second Life residents", *Technovation*, 32(7–8), p. 464-476, 2012.

[CHO 12] CHO Y., HWANG J., LEE D., "Identification of effective opinion leaders in the diffusion of technological innovation: A social network approach", *Technological Forecasting and Social Change*, 79(1), p. 97-106, 2012.

[COA 37] COASE R., *The Nature of The Firm*, New York: Economica, 1937.

[COU 02] COURMONT B., RIBNIKAR D, *Les guerres asymétriques*, Paris: PUF, 2002.

[COV 01] COVA V., COVA B., *Alternatives Marketing*, Paris: Dunod, 2001.

[CRO 10] CROSSAN M., APAYDIN M., "A Multi-Dimensional Framework of Organizational Innovation: A Systematic Review of the Literature", *Journal of Management Studies*, 47(6), p. 1154-1191, 2010.

[CRO 77] CROZIER M., FRIEDBERG E., *L'acteur et le système*, Seuil, 1977.

[DEC 87] DECI E.L., RYAN R.M., "The Support of autonomy and the control of behavior journal of personality and social psychology", *Journal of Personality and Social Psychology*, 53(6), p. 1024-1037, 1987.

[DEJ 97] DE JACQUELOT P., KTITAREFF M., "Internet – la maison au centre de la toile", *Les Echos*, September 15, 1997.

[DEN 13] DENIS-REMIS C., LEBRATY J.-F., PHILIPPE H., "The 2008 anti-French demonstrations in China: learning from a social media crisis", *Journal of Contingencies and Crisis Management*, 21(1), p. 45-55, 2013.

[DEU 58] DEUTSCH M., "Trust and suspicion", *Journal of Conflict Resolution*, 2(4), p. 265-279, 1958.

[DOA 11] DOAN A., RAMAKRISHNAN R., HALEVY A.Y., "Crowdsourcing systems on the World-Wide Web", *Commun. ACM*, 54(4), p. 86-96, 2011.

[DOW 13] DOWNES L., NUNES P.F., "Big-bang disruption", *Harvard Business Review*, 91(3), p. 44-56, 2013.

[EDK 06] EDKINS A.J., SMYTH H.J., "Contractual Management in PPP Projects: Evaluation of Legal versus Relational Contracting for Service Delivery", *Journal of Professional Issues in Engineering Education and Practice*, 132(1), 82-93, 2006.

[ERI 12] ERIKSON R.S., WLEZIEN C., "Markets vs. polls as election predictors: An historical assessment", *Electoral Studies*, 31(3), p. 532-539, 2012.

[FOU 98] FOURNIER S., "Consumers and their brands: developing relationship theory in consumer research", *Journal of Consumer Research*, 24, p. 343-373, 1998.

[FRE 84] FREEMAN R.E., *Strategic Management: A Stakeholder Approach.* Boston, Pitman, 1984.

[FRI 05] FRIEDMAN T.L., *The World Is Flat: A Brief History of the Twenty-first Century*, Penguin Books, 2005.

[GAS 11] GASPOZ C., *Prediction Markets Supporting Technology Assessment*, CreateSpace Independent Publishing Platform, 2011.

[GIL 08] GILLIGAN C., *Une voix différente*, Paris: Champs-Flammarion, 2008.

[GIR 90] GIRIN J., "L'analyse empirique des situations de gestion", in A.C. MARTINET (ed.), *Epistémologies et sciences de gestion*, Paris: Economica, p. 141-182, 1990.

[GLA 00] GLADWELL M., *The Tipping Point: How Little Things Can Make a Big Difference*, Little, Brown and Company, 2000

[GOB 01] GOBÉ M., *Emotional branding: the new paradigm for connecting brands to people*, New York: Allworth Press, 2001.

[GOM 02] GOMBRICH E.H., *L'Art et l'Illusion: Psychologie de la représentation picturale* (6 ed.), Phaidon, 2002.

[GOM 13] GOMEZ P.Y., *Le Travail Invisible: Enquête sur une disparition*, François Bourin Editeur, 2003.

[GOS 03] GOSAIN S., "Looking through a Window on Open Source Culture: Lessons for Community Infrastructure Design", *Systèmes d'Information et Management*, 8(1), p. 11-42, 2003.

[GRA 03] GRANOVETTER M.S., "The strength of weak ties", *The American Journal of Sociology*, 78(6), p. 1360-1380, 1973.

[GUI 10] GUITTARD C., SCHENK E., "Le Crowdsourcing: Une typologie des pratiques d'externalisation vers la foule", *XIXth AIMS Conference*, Luxembourg, 2010.

[HOW 06] HOWE J., "The Rise of Crowdsourcing", *Wired*, 14(6), p. 134-145, 2006.

[KEL 98] KELLY K., *New Rules for the New Economy*, NewYork: Penguin Group – Viking, 1998.

[KER 27] KERMACK W.O., MCKENDRICK A.G., "A Contribution to the Mathematical Theory of Epidemicsm", *Proceedings of the Royal Society of London*, Series A, 1927.

[KIM 09] KIM C., OH E., SHIN N., CHAE M., "An empirical investigation of factors affecting ubiquitous computing use and U-business value", *International Journal of Information Management*, vol. 29, no.6, December 2009.

[KIT 13] KITTUR A., "The Future of Crowd Work", *16th ACM Conference on Computer Supported Coooperative Work*, San Antonio, Texas, 23-27 Feb, 2012.

[KLI 98] KLEIN G., *Sources of Power How People Make Decisions*, Cambridge: MIT Press, 1998.

[KOL 10] KOLAR T., ZABKAR V., "A consumer-based model of authenticity: An oxymoron or the foundation of cultural heritage marketing?", *Tourism Management*, 31(5), p. 652-664, 2010.

[LAG 91] LAGADEC P., *La gestion des crises: outils de décision à l'usage des décideurs*, Paris: McGraw-Hill, 1991.

[LAT 92] LATOUR B., *Aramis ou l'amour des techniques*, Paris: La Découverte, 1992.

[LAZ 00] LAZARUS R.S., "Toward Better Research on Stress and Coping", *American Psychologist*, 2000.

[LEB 03] LE BON G., *Psychologie des foules*, PUF, 2003.

[LEB 09] LEBRATY J.F., "Externalisation ouverte et pérennité: une nouvelle étape de la vie des organisations", *Revue Française de Gestion*, 35/192, 151-166, 2009.

[LEB 08] LEBRATY J.F., LOBRE K., "Externalisation ouverte et pérennité", *Congrès des IAE*, Lille, 2008.

[LEB 10] LEBRATY J.F., LOBRE K., "Créer de la valeur par le crowdsourcing: la dyade Innovation-Authenticité", *Systèmes d'Information et Management*, 15(3), p. 9-40, 2010.

[LEF 10] LEFAIX-DURAND A., POULIN D., BEAUREGARD R., KOZAK R., "Relations interorganisationnelles et création de valeur: Synthèse et perspectives", *Revue Française de Gestion*, p. 205-227, 2006.

[LEF 04] LEFEBVRE P., ROOS P., SARDAS J.C., "Les théories des Communautés de Pratique à l'épreuve: Conditions d'émergence et Organisation des communautés", *Systèmes d'Information et Management*, 9(1), p. 25-48, 2004.

[LOB 12] LOBRE, K., LEBRATY, J.F., "L'open Data: nouvelle pratique managériale risquée?", *Gestion*, 2000(4), p. 103-116, 2004.

[MA 08] MA S., *Mathematical Understanding of Infectious Disease Dynamics*, Singapore: World Scientific Publishing, 2004.

[MAC 99] MACINTOSH A., PRENTICE R.C., "Affirming authenticity: Consulting cultural heritage", *Annals of Tourism Research*, 26(3), p. 589-612, 1999.

[MAR 13] MARCHAND D.A., PEPPARD J., "Why IT Fumbles Analytics", *Harvard Business Review*, 91(1), p. 104-112, 2003.

[MCA 12] MCAFEE A., BRYNJOLFSSON E., "Big data: the management revolution", *Harvard Business Review*, 90(10), p. 61-67, 2012.

[MIN 10] MINGERS J., WHITE L., "A review of the recent contribution of systems thinking to operational research and management science", *European Journal of Operational Research*, 207(3), 1147-1161, 2010.

[MOL 07] MÖLLER K., RAJALA A., "Rise of strategic nets – New modes of value creation", *Industrial Marketing Management*, 36(7), p. 895-908, 2007.

[MOR 10] MORS M., "Innovation in a global consulting firm: when the problem is too much diversity", *Strategic Management Journal*, 31(8), p. 841-872, 2010.

[NOR 93] NORMAN R., RAMIREZ R., "From Value Chain to Value Constellation: Designing Interactive Strategy", *Long Range Planning*, 26(6), p. 151, 1993.

[OST 10] OSTERWALDER A., PIGNEUR Y., *Business Model Generation: A Handbook for Visionaries, Game Changers, and Challengers*, John Wiley & Sons Ltd, 2010.

[PAY 01] PAYNE A., HOLT S., "Diagnosing customer value: Integrating the value process and relationship marketing", *British Journal of Management*, 12(2), p. 159-182, 2001.

[PET 12] PETRICK I.J., MARTINELLI R., "Driving Disruptive Innovation", *Research Technology Management*, 55(6), p. 49-57, 2012.

[RIC 10] RICHTNER A., ÅHLSTROM P., "Organizational Slack and Knowledge Creation in Product Development Projects: The Role of Project Deliverables", *Creativity & Innovation Management*, 19(4), p. 428-437, 2010.

[ROD 10] RODE J., "Truth and trust in communication: Experiments on the effect of a competitive context", *Games and Economic Behavior*, 68(1), p. 325-338, 2010.

[ROU 98] ROUSSEAU D.M., SITKIN S.B., BURT R.S., CAMERER C., "Not so different after all: A cross-discipline view of trust", *Academy of Management Review*, 23(3), p. 393-404, 1998.

[RUI 12] RUIZ E.J., HRISTIDIS V., CASTILLO C., GIONIS A., JAIMES A., "Correlating financial time series with micro-blogging activity", *Proceedings of the Fifth ACM International Conference on Web Search and Data Mining*, Seattle, Washington, 2012.

[SCH 11] SCHENK E., GUITTARD C., "Towards a characterization of crowdsourcing practices", *Journal of Innovation Economics*, 1(7), p. 93-107, 2011.

[SMY 10] SMYTH H., GUSTAFSSON M., GANSKAU E., "The value of trust in project business", *International Journal of Project Management*, 28(2), p. 117-129, 2010.

[SPR 12] SPRADLIN D., "Are you solving the right problem?", *Harvard Business Review*, 90(9), p. 84-93, 2012.

[STA 99] STAR S.L., STRAUSS A.,"Layers of Silence, Arenas of Voice: The Ecology of Visible and Invisible Work", *Computer Supported Cooperative Work*, 8(2), p. 9-30, 1999.

[STE 13] STEMLER A.R.,"The JOBS Act and crowdfunding: Harnessing the power–and money–of the masses", *Business Horizons*, 2013.

[SUR 05] SUROWIECKI J., *La sagesse des foules*, Paris: JC Lattès, 2005.

[TIC 13] TICKNOR J.L., "A Bayesian regularized artificial neural network for stock market forecasting", *Expert Systems with Applications,* 40(14), 5501-5506, 2013.

[UED 09] UEDA K., TAKENAKA T., VÁNCZA J., MONOSTORI L., "Value creation and decision-making in sustainable society", *CIRP Annals - Manufacturing Technology*, 58(2), 681-700, 2009.

[VAN 10] VAN ESS H., "Crowdsourcing: how to find a crowd", *ARD/ZDF Academy*, Germany, 2010.

[VAR 11] VARGAS-DE-LEÓN C., "On the global stability of SIS, SIR and SIRS epidemic models with standard incidence", *Chaos, Solitons & Fractals*, 44(12), 2011.

[VOL 02] VOLKOFF V., *Pourquoi je suis moyennement démocrate*, Editions du Rocher, 2012.

[WAN 13] WANG J., LIU M., LI Y., "Analysis of epidemic models with demographics in metapopulation networks", *Physica A: Statistical Mechanics and its Applications*, 392(7), p. 1621-1630, 2013.

[WEI 07] WEICK K.E., SUTCLIFFE K.M., *Managing the Unexpected: Resilient Performance in an Age of Uncertainty* (2nd ed.), San Francisco: Jossey-Bass., 2007.

[WEL 00] WELCH I., "Herding among security analysts", *Journal of Financial Economics*, 58(3), p. 369-396, 2000.

[WIL 85] WILLIAMSON O.E., *The Economic Institutions of Capitalism: Firms, Markets, Relational Contracting*, New York: The Free Press, 1985.

[WIL 12] WILSON H.J., "You, by the numbers", *Harvard Business Review*, 90(9), p. 119-122, 2012.

[WRI 72] WRINKLE R.L., *Introduction to Bayesian Inference and Decision*, Holt, Rinchart and Winston, 1972.

[WYB 04] WYBO J.L., "Mastering risks of damage and risks of crisis - the role of organizational learning", *International Journal of Emergency Management*, 2(1-2), p. 22-34, 2004.

Websites

Amazon MechanicalTurk	http://www.mturk.com/mturk/welcome
Anti-cybercriminalité	http://www.anti-cybercriminalite.fr
Arrêt Cardiaque	http://www.arretcardiaque.org
Businessleads	https://businessleads.com
CafePress	http://www.cafepress.fr
Chinese government website for fighting corruption	http://www.12309.gov.cn
ClickWorker	http://www.clickworker.com/en

Craigslist	http://www.craigslist.org
Crowdflower	http://crowdflower.com
Crowdstrike	http://www.crowdstrike.com
Daily Journal	http://dailycrowdsource.com
Data Publica	http://www.data-publica.com
Data.gouv.fr France	http://www.data.gouv.fr
Enel	http://data.enel.com
Extractive Industries Transparency Initiative	http://eiti.org/fr
Eyeka	http://www.eyeka.com
Fiverr	http://fiverr.com
Forum international sur la cybersécurité (International forum on cyber security)	http://fic2013.com
France 24 Observers	http://observers.france24.com
Hypios	http://www.hypios.com
Inkling	http://inklingmarkets.com
Innocentive	http://www.innocentive.com
InnovationExchange	http://www.innovationexchange.com
Irantalent	http://www.irantalent.com
Kaspersky	http://ksn.kaspersky.com/fr
Kickstarter	http://www.kickstarter.com
Kisskissbankbank	http://www.kisskissbankbank.com
Lionbridge	http://www.lionbridge.com
List of Projects	http://en.wikipedia.org/wiki/List_of_crowdsourcing_projects
Lulu	http://www.lulu.com
MCC	http://data.mcc.gov

Mechanical Turk	https://www.mturk.com/mturk/welcome
MobileWorks	https://www.mobileworks.com
MyMajorCompany	http://www.mymajorcompany.com
NineSigma	http://www.ninesigma.com
Online CCTV monitering company (fighting crime)	http://www.interneteyes.co.uk
Open Data Paris	http://opendata.paris.fr
Predicti	http://www.predicti.fr
Qmarkets	http://www.qmarkets.fr
Redit	http://www.reddit.com
Tartes Kluger	http://www.tarteskluger.com
Threadless (T-shirts)	http://www.threadless.com
Ulule	http://fr.ulule.com
Ushahidi	http://www.ushahidi.com
Vente-privee	http://www.vente-privee.com
WHP	http://www.whp.fr
Yourencore	http://www.yourencore.com
Zynga	http://zynga.com

Index